Mindful Parenting

(a parent-thesis)

ROBIN PAUC

First published in Great Britain in 2011 by Tinsley House Publications, Tinsley House, Main Road, East Boldre, Hampshire SO42 7WT

Text Copyright © Robin Pauc 2011

The right of Robin Pauc to be identified as the author of this work has been asserted by him in accordance with the Copyright, Designs and Patents Act 1998

This book is sold subject to the condition that it shall not, by way of trade or otherwise, be lent, resold, hired out or otherwise circulated without the publisher's prior written consent.

Cover photo courtesy of Iko (aka Erik Reis)

ISBN-13: 978-1466216778
ISBN-10: 14466216778

***

DEDICATION

To the children that taught me pretty much all I know about the brain.

RAP

CONTENTS

Acknowledgements — i

Introduction — 1

Chapter 1   Kids Rule — 5

Chapter 2   Why Things Go Pair-Shaped — 22

Chapter 3   Breast Is Best — 33

Chapter 4   On Yer Bike — 47

Chapter 5   The World Outside — 62

Chapter 6   The Learning Curve — 76

Chapter 7   England Expects — 92

Chapter 8   Tough Love — 109

Chapter 9   A Tangled Web — 121

Chapter 10   I Spy — 135

Chapter 11   Spot The Difference — 152

Chapter 12   Fixing The Parent — 166

Chapter 13   Fixing The Family — 180

Appendix — 196

Further Reading — 202

Glossary — 203

ACKNOWLEDGMENTS

To Lesley "Grumpy" Laver who worked tirelessly to convert and upload the manuscript to produce the e-book and then with great patience created this paperback while only swearing at Microsoft Word 23 times (mainly under her breath).

INTRODUCTION

In most countries of the world it is necessary to undergo some form of structured training and a formal examination, or least some tuition from a person with experience, before attempting to drive a car on your own. Not so with marriage and parenting. Even if you have had the good fortune to have the most perfect parents in the world, life can throw a spanner in the works when you least expect it. If we return for a moment to the analogy of learning to drive, imagine how it would be if you knew nothing about how a car works – that it needs petrol, oil, etc – had no idea how to control it on the road and no experience of what to do when you hit a patch of ice or suddenly enter dense fog.

Few of us will have cause or motivation to analyse the reason why we decided to live with or marry a particular person and so when pregnancy heralds new life and a host of commitments, subconsciously numerous questions or even doubts can start altering the dynamics of the established relationship. Even if the partnership was indeed made in heaven, the adjustments necessary in order to incorporate the third person into the comfortable and well established routine can at the very least generate minor irritations or major stress once things don't go exactly to plan.

It is now recognised that 20% of children will experience some form of learning or behavioural problem. For the parents of a child with a severe form of developmental delay, the dream can turn into a nightmare, while the child with attention deficit hyperactivity disorder can stretch to the limit the patience of a saint. Although there is most often a history of such conditions in the family giving a genetic probability of such conditions arising, they can come out of the blue and cause not only heartbreak to the parents individually but can lead to destruction of the family dynamics and ultimately marital breakdown.

Life being what it is, not every day can be filled with sunshine and returning to the motoring analogy, we can all hit the odd patch of ice or find ourselves in dense fog unsure as to whether it is best to use full beam or dipped headlights. So it is with parenting, there will be good days and bad days but every now and then we are going to be in a situation where we are not sure what is best or fear we are going to lose control and crash.

The human brain is different in many ways to that of other creatures on the planet but one thing that makes it totally unique is its postnatal development and the extended period of nurturing that the human child requires as a consequence. Whereas a foal can be up on its feet and running - albeit a bit wobbly - within hours of its birth, the human offspring will on average take a year before it takes its first tentative steps. The brain of the chimpanzee – our nearest relative – achieves its adult form by seven months, while our large social brain continues to grow and develop until late into the teens.

This extended period of nurturing requires the minimum of one competent adult, better still the nuclear family – mum, dad and the children - and best of all a good old fashion extended family with numerous relatives on hand to baby-sit or advise when things go awry. There are therefore at least two potential problems here.

Firstly, not just the structure of the family needs to be considered but the motives for the most important elements – mum and dad – coming together in the first place. It has been said that the reason we are attracted to a potential partner is all to do with an image we have in our mind of the ideal (the archetypal) mate. This ideal can be based on a number of factors – hair colour, bra size or a particular look - and probably has elements of both nature and nurture built into it. Also, and I hate to say this but love with all the romance stripped away basically is all to do with a combination of the potential mate fitting most of the criteria for being "ideal" and then – wait for it – a chemical reaction in the brain. I am sorry but that is what it boils down to and it is the same bit of chemistry that triggers the bonding that takes place between mother and child. Clearly a better understanding of both the mechanics of a relationship and the chemistry that holds it together would help us understand how things work and why things can go dramatically wrong.

Secondly, the necessary period of extended nurturing is not without its own inherent problems and we are all too familiar with those haunting images of children in orphanages who have been deprived of the love and stimulation the growing brain must have. Because the human brain is still growing at a foetal growth rate after birth and new brain cells will continue to develop long after birth, it is vulnerable to a variety of both subtle and blatant stressors. Chemical additives in food may retard development or cause bizarre behaviour patterns or bullying at school can lead to the

INTRODUCTION

outward expression of such pain with the child becoming aggressive within the family or tragically be turned inwards leading to the child attempting suicide.

Here we must look at all children and their path from birth to adulthood, considering both how the family unit functions but more importantly, how the brain grows and develops and how this will generate the terrible twos, tantrums, moods, learning difficulties and behavioural issues. We must also consider what may happen as the family expands and how being knocked off the top spot can generate jealousy and some very disturbing behaviour, as well as normal sibling rivalry and challenges to the established pecking order within the family unit.

It is to be hoped that with a better understanding of family dynamics and knowledge of how the brain both develops and functions that the everyday occurrences a parent can both expect or be horrified to experience will become less daunting. As knowledge is often equated with power, this book will hopefully empower many parents to not just understand the anger and frustration that so many children exhibit but also provide the know how to handle it in the short-term for the greatest possible long-term benefit.

RAP.

1 KIDS RULE

What do you have in common with the great apes, elephants, whales and dolphins? Well, they are all very sociable creatures and it is thought that the reason for this is that they all, in common with us, have brains that are proportionally bigger than would be expected and they all share a particular brain cell that no other animal on the planet possesses. Now as far as we know all these other creatures have these very unusual brain cells well established in their brains at the time of birth. Not so with us. We have about 15% of these brain cells at birth but the rest develop between four months and four years after birth.

Not only are these unusual brain cells limited to a handful of species, they are also only found in three small areas of the human brain and what is really interesting is that there are more of these cells on the right side of the brain than the left. Now I know what you are thinking! Well it is just that in most people all the clever stuff like language, maths and theory of music takes place on the left side of the brain, while the right side was thought of as being the more basic emotional side. So, if these brain cells are so special - limited to a few species and just three areas of the human brain –

why not pack them all into the left hemisphere of the brain so that they can help us to do all the stuff that sets us apart from the beast of the field?

Right brain – big picture / Left brain – detailed picture

Before looking at these unusual brain cells in a little more detail and considering what the areas of the brain where they are found actually do, it is necessary to look at one of the basic divisions of labour undertaken by the brain.

The novel right brain

The right side of the brain looks at the big picture, while the left side of the brain focuses in on the detail. That is, the right side of the brain sees the forest while the left side sees the tree, its branches and leaves. Also, anything that is new, be it a situation you find yourself in or a piece of new information, will be dealt with by the right side of the brain initially. Once the right brain has given the new situation the once over and has decided it is safe, the left side of the brain will start looking at the details. Imagine that you are going for a job interview; often a scary situation and you are shown into an office and asked to wait. Your eyes will flicker about scanning the area as your right brain carries out a very rapid risk assessment. The right side of the brain can therefore be thought of as the approach/withdrawal side of the brain. If things are not as expected or if a threat is detected the chances are you will withdraw for your own safety. If, however, the right brain is happy with the new situation it will then hand over control to the left side for a more detailed look around.

It is not just us humans that have what is called lateralised functions. A great many creatures on the planet prefer to use the right side of the brain to monitor their surroundings and many animals use this improved scanning to great advantage in detecting predators and prey. From tiny frogs to giant whales (as evidenced by scars to one side of their massive jaws) it seems there is a definite preference to monitor the world with the left eye and hence right brain, and to attack prey from a particular direction.

The old familiar left brain

The left side of the brain deals with details and things that have been learnt and are therefore familiar. If we return to the office scenario, if you decide things are OK and you are going to stay, then your left brain will look at the books on the shelves and the pictures on the wall. It will also be dominant in the processing and use of pretty well everything that you have learnt. So if you get to the interview itself, the left brain will bring your expertise to your potential new employer while your right brain will continue to make rapid intuitive social appraisals so that you can read social cues and hopefully make appropriate responses.

In most people the left brain is the seat of language and where all the more academic, intellectual activity goes on. However, even though both sides of the brain have to work continuously and in harmony, every 90 minutes or so one side of the brain dominates while the other side takes it easy. This explains why you can drive along a very familiar route and spot an old building you have never seen before – left brain dominant – or have no memory of having driven down a particular road – right brain dominant.

The divided brain

This very definite division of labour helps to explain a very common trait in children both with and without developmental delay and that is a strong preference for routine and surroundings that are familiar. If, as is the case with most children, the right side of the brain is more likely to struggle to develop and mature, then it is better in terms of brain functioning to avoid situations that are new and hence challenging to the right under-functioning brain and stick with the familiar which the left brain can cope with happily.

An unusual history

Way back in 1881 the then famous anatomist Betz described a particular brain cell. Later in 1925 von Economo again described this cell in detail, from which time they were called spindle cells. However, this was of course long before the worldwide web and this discovery remained on the shelf gathering dust until 1995 when Esther Nimchinsky wrote a paper about these brain cells and a particular location where they are found in the human brain. In 1999 she wrote a second paper in which she described the spindle cell as being unique to humans and the great apes. From that point on researchers have renamed these cells as von Economo neurons (VENs) in honour of his great work and have looked at an array of possible functions these cells might perform within the human brain and their paralleled development in the great apes, whales, elephants and dolphins.

A UNIQUE CELL FOR A BIG SOCIAL BRAIN

To date spindle cells / von Economo neurons have been found in:-

Humans

Great Apes :	Orangutan / Gorilla / Chimpanzee / Bonobo (pigmy chimp)
Whales:	Killer / Sperm / Humpback / Fin
Dolphin:	Bottlenose
Elephants:	Indian / African

Functions

It has been suggested that von Economo neurons may function in:-
- the ability to concentrate
- to ignore irrelevant cues
- error correction
- working memory
- appropriate social responses
- how we feel
- self awareness

Malfunctions

It has been suggested that abnormal structure and/or function of von Economo neurons may be a factor in a wide range of conditions including:-
- Depression
- Dementia
- Schizophrenia
- Obsessive compulsive disorder (OCD)
- Phobic states

- Anxiety
- Attention deficit disorder (ADD)
- Attention deficit hyperactivity disorder (ADHD)
- Autism
- Asperger's
- Developmental delay

> **THERE WOULD APPEAR TO BE A SIGNIFICANT RELATIONSHIP BETWEEN FOETAL DISTRESS / BIRTH INTERVENTIONS AND THE OCCURRENCE OF DEVELOPMENTAL DELAY**

Big head

Having a relatively large brain relative to our body size is all very well and gives us as humans the potential for a wealth of creativity but it comes at a cost. Because we are bipeds – walk around on our hind legs – and are the only animal on the planet to do this all the time if we exclude birds. We have a relatively small and pretty rigid pelvis and this is necessary to provide the necessary support for our spine while allowing the legs to move freely but a small pelvis also means a relatively small birth canal. Put simply we have a large brain that needs a large skull to house it and a small birth canal limited by the bones that make up the pelvis.

Together these facts mean there is a limit in terms of structure as to how long a pregnancy can continue if the baby is to pass safely through the birth canal. If the baby gets stuck then an assisted delivery may be necessary – forceps or Ventouse – or an emergency Caesarean section may have to be performed before the baby suffers too much foetal distress. It has been suggested that foetal distress and birth interventions are likely to increase the probability of a delay in the development of the brain.

> Large brains are rare:
> They require vast amounts of fuel
> They take a long time to mature
> This requires extended nurturing
> This in turn requires an extended family
> Being warm-blooded requires more brain power which of itself is highly energy dependant

Born too soon

Being born at 40 weeks is generally OK but it is getting very close to the point where it can no longer work and for many mothers with a small pelvis or a big baby a planned Caesarean or an assisted delivery is essential to survival.

At birth our body is pretty well complete only needing to grow in size, that is, apart from our brain which is still growing at a foetal growth rate and still needing to produce even more brain cells. It has been suggested that ideally the human pregnancy needs to be extended by several months but even if this were biologically possible I cannot imagine too many mothers cheerfully accepting a considerably longer pregnancy. So what is the solution? Is there a compromise? The answer is yes but it comes at a cost. Being born too soon means that there has to be an extended period of nurturing, with the baby initially being totally dependent upon the mother and for years partially dependent upon the family. We call this extended period of nurturing juvenilisation. Although a newborn chimp is totally dependent upon its mother, it will be walking at one month and have an adult brain by seven months. Not so the human infant that does not walk until around one year and whose brain does not finish developing until the late teens.

> Human brain still embryonic in form and development at birth
>
> Most species are fully developed at birth – apes shortly after
>
> Human brain continues to grow at rapid foetal growth rate long after birth
>
> Different rates in different regions

Stress and the developing brain

Von Economo neurons appear to be vital to the normal functioning of the brain and to the development of so many of the functions that make us truly human. As only 15% of these cells are present at birth, the remainder forming in a window between four months and four years after birth, it has been suggested by researchers in the field that they are potentially some of the most vulnerable cells in the brain and as such may suffer in terms of normal development if subjected to stress. It has already been suggested that foetal distress and birth interventions significantly increase the probability of developmental delay, that is, delayed maturation of the brain but could other environmental factors also play a role? There has already been a lot of research into maternal viral infections, controversy over the use of certain vaccines and now the use of e numbers in food production has been placed under the microscope.

Of mice and men

> CHEMICAL MARKERS/SWITCHES ARE COLLECTIVELY KNOWN AS THE EPIGENOME
>
> THEY SWITCH ON AND OFF THE EXPRESSION OF PARTICULAR GENES
>
> EPIGENETICS INTRODUCES THE CONCEPT OF FREE WILL INTO OUR UNDERSTANDING OF GENETICS

Most people will have heard of genes and the work that is being conducted on the human genome but how many people have heard of the epigenome? The epigenome can be thought of as a set of switches that effectively switch on/off the genes. In a beautifully thought out experiment a group of researchers simply changed the diet of a certain type of mouse. The mouse in question, the Agouti mouse, is large, round, yellow and always dies of cancer and/or diabetes. Once the diet was changed and a little niacin (Vit B3) added, the off-spring were found to be small, brown and disease free. If that wasn't enough of a surprise, it was also found that the grandchildren were also small, brown and disease free. For the first time this meant that DNA was not destiny and whether or not genes expressed themselves could be manipulated.

A great many of the genes we possess are concerned with growth and development, that is, they govern when we grow our eyes, ears or limb buds. Similarly, the timing of the continuing development of the brain after birth has to be set and this too is under the control of the epigenome. It has been suggested that a variety of stressors can delay the development of the brain and it could well be that it is the reaction of the epigenome to a particular stressor that causes an epigenetic switch not to be switched on, thus not activating its genes, which in turn would have caused the next stage of brain development to take place.

> **EPIGENETICS REWRITES THE RULES**
>
> **OUR DNA – SPECIFICALLY THE 25000 GENES IDENTIFIED BY THE HUMAN GENOME PROJECT – IS NOW WIDELY REGARDED AS THE INSTRUCTION BOOK FOR THE HUMAN BODY**
>
> **BUT GENES THEMSELVES NEED INSTRUCTIONS FOR WHAT, WHEN AND WHERE TO DO IT**

Keeping it in the family

Are learning problems, behavioural issues and general developmental variations genetic in nature? Well, if there is a family history of any of the above on the mother's side of the family, then there is about a 30% probability that one or more of her offspring could have some aspects of a delay in maturation of the brain. If, however, the history is on the biological father's side then the probability shoots up to over 70%.

Now if we go back to what we were saying about the epigenome and the stressors that potentially can prevent the epigenetic switches from being thrown, it all begins to make perfect sense. We are the only animal on the planet to develop von Economo cells principally after birth, our only birthing strategy is to deliver the child prematurely, as a consequence we have an extended period of nurturing and then we bombard the child and its environment with endless potential stressors. Therefore, if you are genetically susceptible, if you suffer foetal distress, if the family is dysfunctional and if you eat junk food all day, then maybe, just maybe you are going to have a difficult ride through childhood.

> IF THE FAMILY HISTORY IS ON THE MOTHER'S SIDE THERE IS A 32% CHANCE OF ONE OR MORE OFFSPRING EXPERIENCING DEVELOPMENTAL DELAY SYNDROME
>
> IF ON THE FATHER'S SIDE THE % RISES TO MORE THAN 70
>
> THE MAJORITY OF DDS SUFFERERS WILL BE BOYS

The dark side of the brain

Each half – hemisphere – of the brain comes together in the midline forming the medial wall of the brain. Curving round the medial wall of each hemisphere is a very special region of the brain called the cingulate gyrus (see diagram 1). The cingulate gyrus has so far been divided up into five separate areas. At the very front of the medial wall the cingulate gyrus bends like a knee and it has therefore been called the perigenual area (around the knee). Just above this area is the anterior (front) cingulate, behind this the middle cingulate and behind this is the posterior (back) cingulate. The area at the very back of the cingulate is called the retro-splenial area (as it is behind an area called the splenium). Now if you are wondering why you needed to know all that, it is because the von Economo neurons are only found in the anterior cingulate, in a tiny area just below the perigenual area called the anterior insular and an area on the outside surface of the brain.

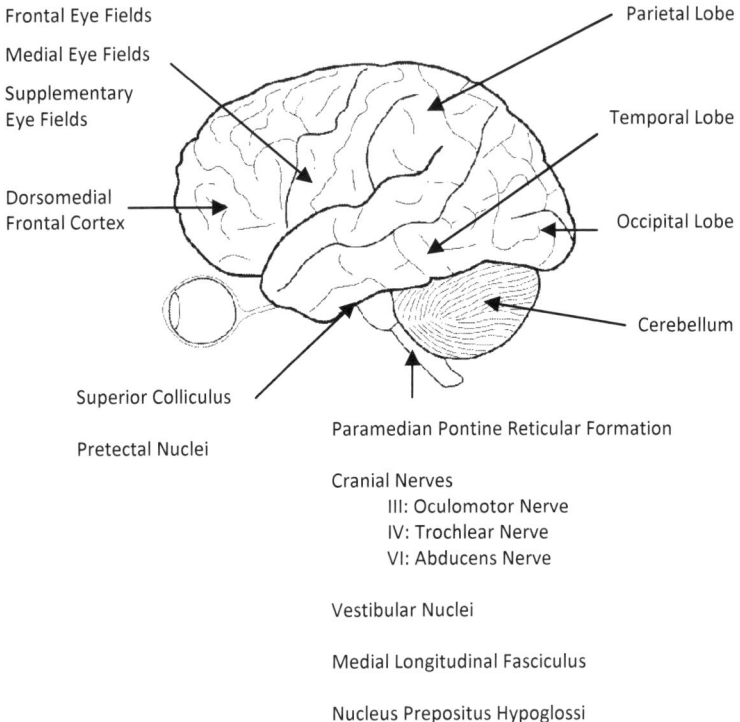

By knowing where the brain cells are and what they do and what the area of the brain where they live does, we can speculate further as to how the brain functions both in sickness and in health. As different areas of the brain have different functions and tend to mature at different rates, then any variation or delay in development can cause a glitch in the behaviour of the perfectly normal child.

The great escape

Let's go back to the anterior cingulate for a moment and this time consider another type of neuron that lives there and that also has a very long name. Calcium-binding Calretinin cells function in the production of facial expression and in aspects of speech. Now what do you think might be happening if the anterior cingulate was having some problems developing as it should and something really stressful like exams were looming up at school? Quite often a child will go through a period of blinking or grimacing, which can be a concern to the child but really freaky to the parents.

When the normal sequence of events in the brain in terms of its development either don't happen or go out of sync two common problems occur. Firstly, something that should happen at a particular age is slow to develop or secondly something that shouldn't happen starts to appear. An example of each of these manifestations will help to explain just what is going on in the brain or rather not going on.

Example 1

A six year old child is struggling to learn to read. Could it be that this child is dyslexic? Or have the areas of the brain which control certain eye movements failed to kick in? In order to read or in fact do anything close up, we need to bring our eyes in towards the nose very accurately. They have to do this very precisely as the image you are looking at has to be projected on to the same area of the retina in each eye. Once having brought the eyes in towards the nose, it is then necessary to hold that convergence while you track smoothly left to right so that you can read. A failure to bring the eyes in towards the nose makes reading a nightmare and makes the possibility of a misdiagnosis of dyslexia very likely.

Example 2

A perfectly normal healthy boy of seven starts blinking and grimacing. It is worse when he is tired and particularly bad when he is under pressure and getting stressed out. Many parents are so concerned that they end up shouting at the child, which only serves to make matters worse or take them off to the GP. So what is happening here? Well returning to the anterior cingulate and those cells with the long name, here we are seeing an example of "escape". Normally in the brain motor nerves (nerves that make movements happen) only fire when they are told to in a very complicated sequence of events. If the anterior cingulate is not functioning precisely as it should, then the Calcium-binding cells can fire spontaneously – escape - and we then get involuntary movements – blinking, grimacing, etc.

Fortunately, both of the examples given above are easily recognised and very easily treated. So, no problem there then but what about the extended period of nurturing that we have to endure while we wait for the brain to grow, develop and mature? Could a better understanding of just how the brain works and a far better understanding of family dynamics smooth the path through infancy, childhood and adolescence? After all we haven't even mentioned yet the terrible twos let alone puberty and the almost overnight transformation of your adorable son into a mindless Kevin.

Knowing what should be happening in the brain and what to do if things go wrong would be of great benefit, as would recognising patterns of events in such things as the developmental milestones that should be ringing bells. Understanding the cause of anger, frustration and tantrums in children at certain stages of development and how to defuse or deal with these outbursts in the sitting room or worse still in the supermarket would not only make life easier for the parent but would also go a long way towards ensuring that the child does not go on to suffer a low level of self esteem and end up as so many kids do, thinking that they are rubbish. Whether you are the proud parent of the most perfect child in the world or if you are the mother that senses that something is not right, understanding how the brain works and what happens when it doesn't, empowers you to put things right.

A glitch or two will happen in every child's life, now you will know the reason why.

CASE HISTORY 1 – Olivia aged 6

Olivia entered the world via an emergency Caesarean section due to foetal distress. However following this early glitch everything fell into place and she attained all her developmental milestones without a problem. In fact everything in the garden was wonderful until one day Olivia's teacher asked if she could have a quiet word with her mother. Again everything in the classroom setting was perfect with the exception of reading and spelling and her teacher was now wondering if she might be dyslexic.

During the consultation it was the possibility of Olivia being dyslexic that her parents focused on, to the exclusion of the very obvious lack of attention and a clear history of dyspraxia. This is not unusual and unless very careful we all have a tendency to see only the obvious. That is, we over focus on a detail while ignoring the big picture.

Following the consultation and examination I explained to the family about how things like dyslexia, dyspraxia and attention deficit always appear in patterns of comorbidity (together) to the point that they should be reclassified as being a presentation of developmental delay. Yes, Olivia was struggling with her reading but she also could not keep her eyes, let alone her metal focus, on anything for more than a few seconds. Her history of being accident prone, clumsy, late learning to dress and learning to pedal a trike might just point to dyspraxia, which was borne out by the examination results.

You may think that this is splitting hairs but if we can identify enough symptoms within a developmental delay, rather than just provide a label, we stand a very good chance of coming up with an effective treatment plan. In the case of Olivia the effective treatment was no more than diet, supplements, simple physical exercises to help the cerebellum and computer generated treatments for her convergence insufficiency and retained primitive defensive visual reflex.

2 WHY THINGS GO PAIR-SHAPED

Before considering the effect / affect a child can have upon a couple and the compromises that are necessarily involved in the transition from being a couple to a family, it is necessary to look at why that couple came together in the first place and whether or not it was for all the right reasons. It is all very well to talk about falling in love and all the other idyllic reasons for living together or indeed getting into wedlock but the fact of the matter is that logical thinking does not play a great part in the decisions we make at such a time and the majority of what does occur will be guided by subconscious images of what is the ideal partner and a lot of chemical jiggery-pokery taking place deep down inside your brain.

> **A LOVE POTION THAT WORKS**
>
> Oxytocin is a hormone and neurotransmitter that is produced in the brain.
>
> As a neurotransmitter – chemical messenger – it is active during falling in love, pair bonding, foreplay, orgasm and **trust**. It also bonds mother and child.
>
> As a hormone it circulates around the body during labour and breastfeeding

Love is blind and why we not only find someone attractive but fall in love with them is as a consequence a mystery, or is it? It has been suggested that a combination of nature – your genes – and nurture – your life experiences – will together help to form in your subconscious brain an image of the ideal partner. This "ideal" partner is the living flesh and blood of what your mind has created and has been called an archetype. The image held within the brain will rule out certain hair colours, pale skin, body forms and will even find certain natural body odours an absolute turn off. The "ideal" image that we have is so coloured that we do not give a second glance to anyone not fitting the basic image and tiny sensors in the nose (vomeronasal organs) may even send subtle but very definite messages to the more primitive areas of the brain saying a silent but nevertheless resounding "No".

The computer says "No"

Whether or not you believe in the teachings of Darwin, what we try to achieve in the short-term, is at least genetic compatibility and then hopefully in the long-term, genetic immortality. That is, if we are fortunate enough to have children, grand-children, great grandchildren, etc., etc. then our genes live on as the family tree grows and we genetically, at least, exceed our three score years and ten. Genetic compatibility is not only a thing that is guided by our silent mentor but is also built into the written and unwritten laws of most societies thus making the marriage of close relatives unlawful. Our silent mentor often does not employ logic or personal experience but nevertheless make explicit judgements as to what is right and what is wrong. Take the following example of a test question from the field of neuropsychology:-

A brother and sister are on holiday in the South of France having both graduated from university. After a sumptuous meal and perhaps a little too much wine they find themselves in each other arms and make love. She is on the pill and he uses a contraceptive, therefore the likelihood of her becoming pregnant is remote. Is this act of love/bonding acceptable or not?

The chances are that regardless of your religious, cultural or educational background you will find the act unacceptable to say the least or totally repulsive. But ask yourself why? The answer is, it just is. Built into our deepest unconscious mind is a taboo that says incest is wrong and therefore we have to have a moral code that prevents interbreeding and promotes genetic compatibility and ultimately survival. But what else can sway us to "fall in love", what other hidden powers can move us and are our motives always pure?

You cheeky monkey

Research into the behaviour of monkeys has come up with some interesting results that could go a long way towards explaining pair-bonding in general but also some of the more unlikely relationships we read about in the newspapers. Serotonin is another neurotransmitter that is found both in the gut where it helps to get things moving and in the brain where it functions in memory, learning, mood, appetite and movement. Now, certainly in monkeys, a low serotonin level is associated with low social status, while a high serotonin level is associated to a high level of success in attracting a mate.

SEROTONIN AND RISK TAKING

High levels of serotonin = higher status, being relaxed, confident and socially stable

Low levels of serotonin = anti-social behaviour & risk taking

Low serotonin monkeys found new food sources and served as sentries (high risk job)

Alerting the group to danger puts low serotonin monkeys at risk but helps ensure the survival of high serotonin monkeys

Is this genetic survival via neurotransmitters?

Also, while high serotonin levels increase the likelihood of prosocial behaviour, – fitting into society – low levels are associated with increased risk taking and perhaps antisocial behaviour. It has even been suggested that from an evolutionary standpoint that an individual with low serotonin levels and having attention deficit hyperactivity disorder would have been an asset to the hunting party as they would be less likely to see danger and therefore more likely to act impulsively and kill the prey.

You may not have heard of serotonin before but the chances are that you will be more than a little familiar with cholesterol and how high levels of cholesterol in the blood increases the risk of heart disease. But did you also know that low levels of cholesterol are associated with an increased probability of a violent death due to an accident or suicide. Also, and here's the link, low cholesterol levels are associated with more aggressive behaviour and lower levels of serotonin. As low serotonin levels lead to increased food seeking and risk taking, the likelihood of obtaining energy rich food – cholesterol – increases, thus restoring the balance in the short-term at least.

CHOLESTEROL

It has been suggested that seeking high energy foods may be a retained behaviour pattern to ensure high cholesterol levels and thereby serotonin.

But in the modern societies where high energy foods are in abundance this may lead to an increased risk of heart disease and obesity.

So having a high serotonin level increases not just your chances of bonding but it also goes a long way towards explaining the unlikely couples we mentioned before. But it is not just serotonin levels that are going to significantly influence your chances of pulling. Status, power and a mega bank balance can also tip the balance in a more structured society. Status and power often go hand in hand with wealth but you don't need to be famous if you are loaded. For some people just being seen with the rich and famous is enough to fulfil a primitive desire to be noticed, to be recognised for something, anything. For others the need for not just the luxurious living that accompanies wealth but the financial security such a liaison brings with it is all important to them. It is tempting to suggest that the beautiful young woman that marries an elderly millionaire is no more than a high-class tart but for some at least it is true love – at least as far as their neurotransmitters are concerned.

Sometimes love is not blind, in fact, it is not love at all just plain lust. I hate to say this but every now and then, and yes, it is usually us guys, we think we are in love when in fact we have airbrushed the image in our mind to such a point that we fall in lust with a false image. Love, as we will see later can be transient but lust is shallow, possibly highly enjoyable at the time but inevitably short lived. We are all familiar with the scenario in which the man sees the woman of his dreams and instantly falls in lust, that is, until she opens her mouth and utters those immortal words "What you looking at, you perv". It is perhaps wise to remember that all show often equals no go. But in defence of the man who does not think with his brain nor even his heart but a region a little further south, it is necessary to remember that not all creatures can be monogamous as doves and that for some individuals there is a powerful unconscious drive to impregnate as many females as possible. This basic drive is not romantic and to many may sound like an excuse for philandering but I am afraid in terms of basic animalistic behaviour it is a fact of life. Genetic survival and that is survival of the fittest genes not only depends upon successful impregnation but also the widest possible coverage of the gene pool.

Mr Right and why the Mrs Left?

The individual, it has been said, is a point on the line of history where it is bisected by biography. History is time and time waits for no man therefore the person you marry today for all the right reasons – archetype + hormones + neurotransmitters – is not necessarily going to be the same person ten years down the line of history. So what can go wrong and just what causes the marriage made in heaven to end up in the divorce from hell?

An affair of the heart?

Perhaps the most common reason that a marriage ends is because one partner is unfaithful. This can be due to a variety of causes but the most common are most likely a reduction in physical relations once the honeymoon period is over, sexual incompatibility, boredom or the unconscious need to supply the gene pool and gain a neurotransmitter high in the process.

In sickness and in health?

A change in the physical health of a partner can place a huge strain on a relationship. This does not just mean in terms of a reduction or cessation of physical relations, although the physical and mental stress this can build up can be a real strain but the immediate and long term changes it can bring in terms of expectations within the relationship.

A child born with a disability or a child that goes on to develop attention deficit hyperactivity disorder or Tourette's syndrome can place unbearable strain upon even the best relationship and without respite can drive a couple apart as they seek a return to normality, an escape from the certainty the day will bring.

For richer, for poorer

During the good times even a rocky relationship can work but when poverty knocks at the door, love can very quickly fly out the window. It takes a strong bond to survive the hard times and sometimes it is not strong enough and a partner leaves looking for a return to the good life and/or greater financial security.

Not the man I married

Evolving and changing as a person can be a life enriching process but in some relationships it can be a step too far. Education, ambition or simply a need for change can drive couples apart as expectations rise, interests widen or the need to succeed outweighs everything. At a more subtle level, those few extra pounds and not taking a pride in your appearance anymore can chip away at the foundations of a long term relationship.

Once the nest is feathered

Many young ladies dream of finding Mr Right, getting married, buying a house and having babies. If the dream comes true and the happy couple are blessed with two wonderful children, can we be sure that all those brain chemicals that made it all possible in the first place will go on being produced and thereby maintain the status quo? The answer is I suspect that once the biological needs have been fulfilled the levels of the neurotransmitters may drop dramatically. Should this happen and I would suggest it is the norm, then all the things that the transmitters caused to occur – mate-bonding, love, sex, orgasm and trust – can diminish or stop altogether. How many women would admit to not only not loving their partner anymore but actually not even liking them? How many partners stay together for the sake of the children but in doing so provide the worse possible role model, in which resentment replaces love and constant bickering is the order of the day or worse still when communication breaks down altogether and long periods of silence ensue?

Having looked at the fundamentals of the relationship, certainly as it occurs within the Western world, it is now time to move on to the tricky subject of parenting. It is said that two's company and three is a crowd and unless child number one was a joint decision trouble could already be brewing. Although, "Guess what darling?" can be the sweetest words a husband can hear and via oxytocin strengthen bonds, if pregnancy and the switch to family life wasn't in the game plan it can be the beginning of the end and the path to being a single mother. A solo decision to try for a baby and a feeble excuse as to how it could have happened really isn't going to work in this day and age and is possibly a very good recipe for disaster. Remember how the word trust was very much associated with oxytocin and how it is this transmitter that is the glue that bonds the relationship. Such deceit can cause wounds that never heal and may continue to fester for the duration of a marriage insidiously gnawing away at the very fabric of all that was potentially so good.

We will return to and consider in more detail the impact the child can have upon pair-bonding and indeed how the needs and expectations of the couple are met collectively and singly by the new arrival and perhaps more importantly how this will effect/affect the life that is to unfold before them. As we follow events from pregnancy to puberty, we will as far as possible look at how such events can help or hinder development and how both good and bad behaviour can be related to specific areas of the brain.

The parents of a child with a learning disability or behavioural problems will often assume that whatever the child does is because of their problem and not realise that all children will be naughty at times, and need guidance and boundaries as they follow the path through childhood to adolescence. Conversely, the parent blessed with the child that is an angel can be horrified when one day he throws a wobbly, develops some very peculiar habits or starts blinking and grimacing. Here the question is what is normal and the answer invariably will lie in the postnatal development of the brain and the fluctuations that can occur in that development and maturation set against the expected targets we call developmental milestones.

Even before the foetus makes the journey towards infancy and the great outdoors, factors can be at play that will potentially alter their development and the journey itself is not without its own inherent dangers. The effects of smoking, drinking and drug abuse during pregnancy have been well documented and a lot of research has looked at maternal stress and the impact it may have upon the developing foetus. Further research has suggested a link between foetal distress and the increased probability of development delay. Foetal distress can occur when the baby simply cannot exit the womb due to its presentation, when it gets stuck in the birth canal, when it has the cord around its neck or when it has a bowel movement prior to delivery.

Birth interventions, notably the forceps and Ventouse assisted delivery would appear to be significant factors in raising the probability of a delay in the normal development of the brain. In one study it was found that children that had suffered foetal distress were four times more likely to have developmental delay, while those delivered by a Ventouse assisted delivery were ten times more likely. Another study found that 42% of children delivered by this method had blood in their cerebrospinal fluid suggesting an intracranial haemorrhage.

Maternal stress during the delivery may cause raised levels of adrenaline – the stress hormone – in the blood. As adrenaline acts against oxytocin, the level of oxytocin in the maternal blood may drop significantly. This may lead to a cascade of events including the reduced strength of uterine contractions, leading to an increased length of labour, leading to an increased probability of an assisted delivery.

Stress caused to the mother and baby during an assisted delivery and raised levels of adrenaline have been implicated in causing reduced oxytocin levels which may delay the outset of lactation and less frequent sucking in the infant. As we will see later, problems latching-on and reduced suckling may herald further problems down the line and have been found to be associated with delayed speech and/or chewing.

3 BREAST IS BEST

> AS SOMEBODY ONCE SAID: BREAST MILK CONTAINS ALL THE RIGHT INGREDIENTS, IS ALWAYS AT THE RIGHT TEMPERATURE AND COMES IN ATTRACTIVE CONTAINERS

The onset of lactation is under the control of two hormones - prolactin and oxytocin. As oxytocin levels can be reduced in response to raised levels of adrenaline, it follows that a stressful birth may delay the onset of milk production. The initial milk is referred to as colostrum and this helps to protect the baby until its own immune system is functioning. It also helps to expel the meconium (contents of the bowels) as it has a mild laxative effect, as opposed to breast milk proper which reduces the likelihood of diarrhoea. It has also been suggested that the breastfed child is less likely to suffer from asthma, eczema and ear infections, with which the parents of a child with a developmental delay will be all too familiar.

There would appear to be a link between problems latching on to the nipple and the ability to suckle normally and delays in the onset and normal development of speech. Some children go on to be fussy-eaters and restrict their diet to foods that do not require chewing. This may well be due to a reduced awareness of where the tongue is and late development of the control of movements, which would not only make the production of speech very difficult but could only potentially lead to the tongue being bitten and hence the reluctance to chew. It is essential for both parents and professionals to pick up on these early clues as both effective parenting and treatment should it be necessary needs, like a jigsaw puzzle, to have as many pieces in place as possible to make the going easier.

Written in stone

The developmental milestones we now need to consider are sitting unaided, crawling, walking, talking and bladder control. The average infant should be able to sit unaided by around six months. The floppy baby may be a little later but delays by a few months may herald further delays in crawling and walking. Between six to ten months the infant should start to crawl on all fours. A delay in crawling might follow late sitting but crawling for only a brief time, not crawling, combat crawling and bottom shuffling may be early signs of problems with normal movement development and can be the earliest signs that the child will go on to struggle with both gross – using your body - and fine – using your fingers – motor control. Often children that have delayed milestones or skip crawling altogether will go on to have problems learning to dress themselves and be delayed in such things as riding a bike.

The importance of crawling is thought to be to do with establishing within the spinal cord what are called interneurons – small connecting neurons – particularly in the neck and low back regions. In these two regions we have to create what have been called central pattern generators. When we decide to do a one-off movement like scratching an itch, we have to send a specific message from the area of the brain that has made the decision through a complicated loop deep within the brain before instructions to the muscles that will carry out the movement can be sent down the spinal cord. If we had to do that in order to take a simple step we would progress at a snails pace. Instead, for any learnt rhythmic movements the initial command to start walking enters the loop but then branches off and is sent down to the central pattern generators that then fire up the necessary muscles in the correct sequence. Hence not crawling can be a sign of troubles ahead.

Walkies

The average infant makes the transition into being a toddler at roundabout one year. Apart from being the time when nothing is safe in the house anymore, it is also an important developmental stage. A delay at this stage of more than two months may indicate developmental delays happening upstairs. A slow start in getting going may not be anything to worry about at all but when put together with early clues might mean that extra attention needs to be paid to what happens next in terms of speech development etc, plus it may be worthwhile ensuring that everything that can be done to help with the development of the brain is put in place.

Perhaps of a little more concern is the child that rushes through the early stages or even skips crawling altogether and much to the mother's delight is walking months before he/she should. There is a normal, natural pruning back process that should take place in the brain and it has been suggested that if this does not take place the brain may fail to process information as it should and the child may at least initially become a concrete thinker, taking everything literally. Early walking may be a sign that this process has not been completed. Similarly, the child that is into everything at this stage may continue to be very, if not hyperactive, which may be suggestive of an under-functioning region of the medial wall.

Once the child becomes a toddler, a primitive reflex called the Babinski response should be lost, to be replaced with the adult response. If you stroke the sole of an infant's foot the toes should go up. Once the toddler is up and away the response to having the sole stroked should be the opposite – adult form – and they should claw down. In one study it was found that 46% of children with developmental delay – a mixture of dyslexia, dyspraxia, attention deficit, etc. – had the infantile response. This is called a retained reflex, and again, in children may suggest that the brain is not maturing at the normal rate.

Talkies

As a rule of thumb the average child will be able to use single words in the first year, two words together – me go, you come – in the second year and mini sentences in the third year of life. Certainly in the UK any problems with speech development should be picked up at an early stage and a referral for a speech therapy assessment put in place. However, every now and then the odd child that is tongue-tied slips through the net and it is always worth checking to see if the child can raise their tongue to the roof of the mouth yourself. Also, when doing this simple test it is a golden opportunity to see if the child that is having a speech delay or problem can move the tongue from side to side inside the mouth. If the child protrudes the tongue it could be that the child has little control over the movement of the tongue and may have an oral / verbal dyspraxia. This may not only impact upon the child's ability to learn to speak clearly but may also have a knock-on effect and causing feeding issues.

Some children start the process of acquiring language and often after running a temperature for a day or two, lose the speech they have acquired. Now there is no hard evidence for this but it seems to happen most frequently about the time of the MMR. Hard evidence there may not be but the anecdotal evidence is certainly enough to make you want to stop and think. We talked earlier about the epigenome and the control it has over development and how stressors might just prevent the switches being thrown or even switch off a gene that has already been triggered. It is no more than a thought but could some children be more susceptible, sensitive if you like, to vaccines and might it not be a good idea to screen all children prior to vaccinating them? After all it has to be cheaper to carry out a simple screening test than it is to care for a child with a severe developmental delay and think of the heartbreak it might prevent.

Food for thought

Any time from four to six months the child will be offered solids. As to when varies around the country with what would appear to be a North/South divide. This is the time to start the basics of a balanced diet and sensible eating patterns but it is also the potential starting point of a catalogue of problems ranging from actually getting food into the infant to childhood obesity. Food allergies are not uncommon and some infants even react at the milk stage. Real food intolerances on the contrary are not that common although some children with more severe delays can find certain textures and tastes very unpleasant. In practice, most often the child that supposedly has severe food intolerances, as described by his mother, has no problems whatsoever with cereals, crisps, sweets, chocolate and burgers. Strange that.

The balancing act

To provide a balanced diet requires little more than common sense. The first meal of the day is literally the time that we break the fast, having gone through the longest gap between meals in the 24 hour cycle. For children, this can be 12 hours plus and therefore the first meal of the day after the fast should not be based on processed carbohydrates – toast or cereals. Apart from the fact that many breakfast cereals are laced with salt and have a high sugar content, the body will digest this type of food in minutes tempting the child to feel the need for a little grazing mid morning. Therefore, it is better to start the day with a combination of protein, fat and carbohydrate so that the digestive system can be occupied for a longer period of time.

The mid morning snack if required can be an apple which should keep most children happy until lunch time. A packed lunch or school dinner – if good – will continue the good work of trying to keep the digestive system ticking-over in order to reach and maintain our goal of keeping the blood sugar level as steady as possible. Some children and notably those with problems of hyperactivity will crave sugars and recent research has suggested that children can be addicted to sugar in the same way as young adults can become addicted to hard drugs. The best time for sugar addiction cold turkey is now.

Once school is over a portion of fruit or carrot sticks and dips will keep up the good work but may need to be supplemented if the child is attending any after school activities. The evening meal should be home cooked, prepared from scratch and should include at least three vegetables. Providing carrots or broccoli every day because they are the only vegetables they will eat is a big mistake. You will be amazed at the quantity of spinach a child will eat once they have got the taste for it.

Young children will often lean forward and smell a meal before attempting to eat it or refusing point blank. This is a primitive and very normal activity that we all do to some extent when presented with something we are not familiar with even though we sometimes pretend we are just savouring the aroma. There is a theory that if a child sees and smells a new food 50 times they are likely to eat it. The right side of the brain is where we think about smells and once the right side of the brain is familiar with the smell it will hand over the decision to try the new food to the left side of the brain.

It is essential to make sure that young children drink enough during the day. While the child is in your care this should not present a problem as water can be provided with each meal and they can be offered a drink every time you have one. Once the child is left in the care of others, things can go awry and bad habits develop. A trendy, colourful water bottle and a great deal of nagging if the bottle comes home full may be all that is required to establish a healthy habit that should last a lifetime. When children become dehydrated they do not function at their best and anyone who has suffered a hangover will know exactly what I mean.

Serial adverts

The next time you have the opportunity or misfortune to have to watch the television for a long period of time note how many adverts there are for cereals and processed foods. While doing this note how few adverts there are for healthy foods and how the government actually has to remind us to eat our five a day, reduce fats and take exercise. Clearly it is going to be a losing battle all the time the manufacturers of cereals and junk food are allowed to spend millions convincing our children that chocolate breakfast cereals and burgers are the things to eat while the poor old government faced with the literally growing problems of obesity, diabetes and heart disease struggle to come up with anything that is going to convince an overweight ten year old boy to dump the junk.

Oil can

Something in the region of 60% of the human brain is fat and of that fat 20% has to be essential fatty acids. These fatty acids – the omegas – are called essential not just to make them sound important as in the essential fashion accessory but because the brain cannot grow, develop, mature and maintain itself without them. As a child's brain is growing at a phenomenal rate and will continue to grow and develop late into the teens, it obviously needs the omegas in the right quantities on a daily basis. Now the chances are that no matter how good your diet is you will not be supplying, certainly omega 3, in sufficient quantities to fulfil the requirements of the very demanding brain. And it is not just children that are potentially missing out on the essential dietary requirements. The Mental Health Foundation has stated that there may be insufficient omega 3 in the average adult diet and this could be a contributing factor in a wide variety of mental illnesses.

Mineral rights

Various studies carried out around the world have found that a significant number of children are suffering from mineral deficiency either through low dietary intact or due to a reduced ability to process them within the body. Iron deficiency in children is not uncommon and strangely enough may be exacerbated by drinking too much cows milk. Should you suspect your child may be iron deficient you should speak to your GP.

Symptoms of iron deficiency in children may include:-
- Fatigue
- Headache
- Irritability
- Pale skin
- Getting out of breath
- Decreased appetite

Both zinc and magnesium deficiencies have been linked to the occurrence of developmental delay and particularly to an increased incidence of attention deficit hyperactivity disorder (ADHD). Some researchers have found localised pockets in various countries where a great number of children fulfil the criteria for having ADHD and have related this to dietary deficiency of these minerals. It has also been suggested; particularly when the diet has been poor, that vitamins B complex and C should be added to the diet as a supplement. However, it is essential to ensure that children under 12 years have an age appropriate dose and that the products used are free from artificial sweeteners and bad e numbers.

Meet to eat

With the advent of convenience foods and the microwave oven it has become possible to produce meals in minutes and this has led to many mothers pandering to their children's whims and providing a different meal for each child. As if this is not bad enough, often the meals will be consumed at different times and in different places. Whenever possible the family should sit down together at the table and eat together. This is not only a great time to catch up on the events of the day but also provides the ideal opportunity to fine tune table manners and behaviour in general. It also provides an opportunity to observe any problems a child may be having deciding which hand to hold the knife and fork in and how well your child is coping with the whole tricky business of eating nicely. Problems with handedness and being a messy eater, wearing your food, can again be early signs of a brain struggling to develop or be further evidence of dyspraxia.

A problem that is weighing down the nation

Obesity in general is increasing at a frightening rate but childhood obesity has now become a national concern with predictions that if it continues many children will die before their parents. There was a joke going around, if you can call it that, that you could see a rise in obesity with the opening of the first fast food outlet in a country and parallel its rise to the number of new outlets opening. Again, think of the millions of pounds / dollars that are spent annually convincing our children to go for a burger and fries and ask yourself why? Yes, they're loving it but at what cost to you?

It is a known fact that the brain needs fat but it has to be the right fat if the brain is to grow and function correctly. If the brain can't get the right fats it will have to make do with whatever is available. Studies have shown that if you are persistently overweight - which may well suggest not only the ingestion of too many calories but perhaps a junk food diet – you decline mentally as well as physically. A recent study using MRI scanning technology helped to explain this mental decline by showing that over time the brain literally starts to shrink. We used to say "You are what you eat" but perhaps now we should say "You are not what you were when you eat junk".

A weight off my mind

Very, very few people on the planet have a medical condition that makes them grossly overweight. Being big boned does not contribute in any significant way to the several stones that need to be shed. The excuse of "He's a growing boy" is no excuse for providing a child with adult sized portions and/or allowing the child to raid the cupboards or fridge at will.

If your child is overweight there is a significantly increased risk of:-
- Diabetes
- Heart disease
- Problems sleeping
- Asthma
- Raised blood pressure
- In girls early puberty
- Long term – increased risk of cancer and/or premature death

Leading by example

It will probably come as no great surprise to you to learn that there is an increased probability that if you are significantly overweight then the chances are that so will your children. It would perhaps be comforting to some to say that this is of course genetic but the truth of the matter probably lies in the consumption of junk food, portion size, snacking and insufficient exercise. Parenting is not just about putting a roof over their heads and making sure they have the latest iPod, it is all about leading by example and that should not include leading them to an early grave.

Body Mass Index

Most people these days have access to the internet and providing you have the following information to hand you can quickly find out if your child is at risk:-

1. Gender
2. Age
3. Height
4. Weight

Simply Google Calculate Body Mass Index Children (BMI) type in the required information and the BMI will pop up immediately. Most sites will provide you with values similar to those shown below.

Underweight = <18.5

Normal weight = 18.5-24.9

Overweight = 25-29.9

Obesity = BMI of 30 or greater

To pee or not to pee

As a general rule most children will have gained bladder control by day by the third year and at night shortly afterwards but it is not unusual particularly with boys for this to be delayed. In the infant and toddler when the bladder fills to a certain point a message is sent to the spinal cord which then sends a message back to the sphincter – tap – to allow the urine to be voided and hence the need for nappies. After round about two years of age when the message is sent from the full bladder to the spinal cord, rather than sending a message back to open the tap, a message gets sent up to the brainstem and from there to the bladder control executive – the micturition centre. It is at this stage that the child has a conscious awareness of needing to go to the toilet and gradually develops bladder control by day.

Gaining bladder control by night usually takes a little longer as sometimes the executive in control of the bladder is in such a deep sleep that the brainstem can't get a decision about what to do and eventually tells the spinal cord to deal with it. As the centre for executive control of the bladder lies just above areas of the brain that are often involved in behavioural issues, a delay in gaining bladder control may provide yet another clue that the brain is not developing as quickly as it should. Bedwetting is twice as common in boys with as many 10% of five year olds having problems at night.

Parents with concerns about persistent bedwetting usually seek advice from their GP and may be referred on to a specialist clinic for advice and treatment. However, if the bedwetting is a symptom of developmental delay it usually ceases once the other issues have been addressed. Anxiety and stress may cause episodes of bedwetting and should alert the parent to the need for some very sympathetic and very necessary probing to unearth the underlying cause. The sudden onset of bedwetting in a child that has been consistently dry should alert the parent to the possibility of bullying or abuse.

Eye contact

Some children struggle to make good eye contact and this in combination with other signs can be of great concern and may indicate autistic traits. Other children make limited eye contact and tend to prefer familiar faces. Restricted eye contact may be indicative of a child that's a little shy but is more likely to be a sign that the right side of the brain is not maturing perhaps as quickly as it might. In somewhat older children a retained primitive visual reflex that forces the eye to look at anything that appears or moves in the peripheral visual fields may be interpreted wrongly as being attention deficit.

CLUES TO DATE

Family history of learning / behavioural problems
Maternal / foetal distress
Birth intervention
Problems latching on
Problems feeding
Speech delay
Delayed sitting/crawling/walking
Poor gross / fine motor skills
Delayed bladder control
Bedwetting
Poor eye contact

4 ON YER BIKE

Once you have found your feet, the world becomes your oyster and during the exploration that follows it becomes increasingly necessary to gain an amazing repertoire of both gross and fine motors skills. Although most of us are not going to become tightrope walkers, it is important in everyday activities – walking, feeding, writing, using tools - to be at least competent if not skilful. As the learning/behavioural problems never occur in isolation and dyspraxia is the most common comorbid (appearing together) symptom, any signs of dyspraxic tendencies may be an early warning sign of problems to come.

Dyspraxia can take many forms and vary considerably in the degree to which it is manifested, therefore it can insidiously be built into the characteristic behaviour of a child, which unrecognised can plague the individual for a lifetime and potentially cause a variety of ills – flat feet, backache and accidents. In childhood unrecognised dyspraxia can be the cause of frustration of sudden outbursts of anger and may be the cause of the child being bullied at school.

POSSIBLE SIGNS OF BULLYING

In childhood:
- Mood swings
- Bedwetting
- Outbursts
- Sleep disturbances

In adolescence:
- Female – Uncharacteristic violence
- Male – Excessive alcohol consumption

Dyspraxia is the inability to learn easily or perform smoothly a movement or series of movements necessary to complete a desired task. This can cause a child to be a messy eater, to say "I am rubbish at sports" or simply be a disaster waiting to happen. We are all familiar with such expression as – a bull in a china shop, cack-handed or having two left feet – and in many ways we just accept that some people are clumsy by nature, when in fact poor spatial awareness and dyspraxic tendencies should be identified and addressed at an early age, not just blindly accepted. Being dyspraxic on the outside often means low self esteem on the inside which may be the cause of untold suffering and the reason behind the sudden outburst or tantrum.

> **GROUNDED**
>
> In order to be able to stand on your own two feet it is necessary to be what is called "grounded". That is, upright, confident and perfectly balanced. Get a child to walk upstairs blindfolded, with their hands by their side and head upright or place yourself on a narrow mountain path with a thousand foot drop on one side. If they or you are not "grounded", you very soon will be as your brain is thinking about survival making you falter, bend, and head for the ground.

Finger food

With most children once they start to feed themselves there is a simple progression from fingers, to spoon, to knife and fork. The child that prefers to continue to use their fingers just might be trying to tell you something and the child that wears their food with pride is providing a sure sign that something is awry. The use of cutlery requires ever increasing levels of motor skills and manual dexterity but also is critical when issues with handedness can come to light. The vast majority of people will end up being right-handed, right-footed and right eye dominant but sometimes the wires get crossed and a mixed dominance may provide important clues as to how the brain is developing.

Checking for eye dominance

Offer the child a toy telescope and assuming they know what it is, see which eye they choose and continue to use. It is generally assumed that if you are right-handed it is the left side of the brain that controls the right hand. Although, the left side of the brain does indeed control the right arm, recent research would suggest that it is the right side of the brain that actually controls the right hand and that control in part comes from an area of the brain that lies immediately behind an area that is well known for being the site where problems with attention originate. As the bulk of developmental issues will be due to problems with the right side of the brain, then poor handwriting in a right-handed individual may be a further clue as to how the brain is growing and maturing.

Addressing dyspraxia

Initially children need to be dressed and undressed but very quickly they start to help out by moving their limbs and before we know it should make a start on firstly undressing perhaps at bath time and then making an attempt at dressing. This is a time when a dressing dyspraxia may become apparent or of more concern, problems in sequencing, as in what to put on first, comes to light. Some children will make a pig's ear out of putting on their trousers while others can take years to learn how to cope with buttons and laces.

Moving on

Most children start the more advanced balancing acts of life by progressing from scooter, to tricycle, to bicycle. As riding a bicycle requires not just the ability to balance but also the necessity to pedal, steer, brake and look where you are going all at the same time, a delay in gaining such coordination may provide yet another clue that things are not progressing quite as they should.

We are all familiar with the expression, keeping one's eyes on the ball, but for some children this is a real problem, sometimes due to not being able to remain focused on the task but very often as the essential skill of hand-eye coordination is lacking. Many young children lack visual focus and sometimes due to a primitive retained visual reflex are distracted by anything that moves around them other than the ball, while others lack mental fixation which also causes them to take their mind's eye off the ball.

Generally when we are learning to catch a ball we start off using both hands and as moving the arms to the required position and closing the hands around the ball needs both accuracy and perfect timing, a great deal of practice is required before we nail the skill. For some children acquiring the skill can seem to take forever or simply does not happen. How many parents have found cause to say "Butter fingers!" on more than one occasion?

At the bottom of the brainstem, on each side, is a small nucleus – a collection of neurons that function as a unit – that pulsate spontaneously. Ideally the nuclei should pulsate equally at between 8-12 Hz. The pulsation passes from the nucleus to the cerebellum on the opposite and from there to the top of the brainstem opposite before passing back down to the nucleus of origin. One of the functions of this circuit is to turn-on / turn-off the motor system on the same side of the body as the nucleus. If you have ever noticed someone's crossed leg bobbing up and down, this is the reason. Now, I said ideally the two nuclei should pulsate at the same rate. Can you imagine what might happen if the two nuclei are way out of sync? The all important timing of bringing the hands together at precisely the right time is not going to happen and the ball will be dropped but also anything that requires the two hands to perform different acts in the same timeframe – doing up a button – is going to be a real struggle.

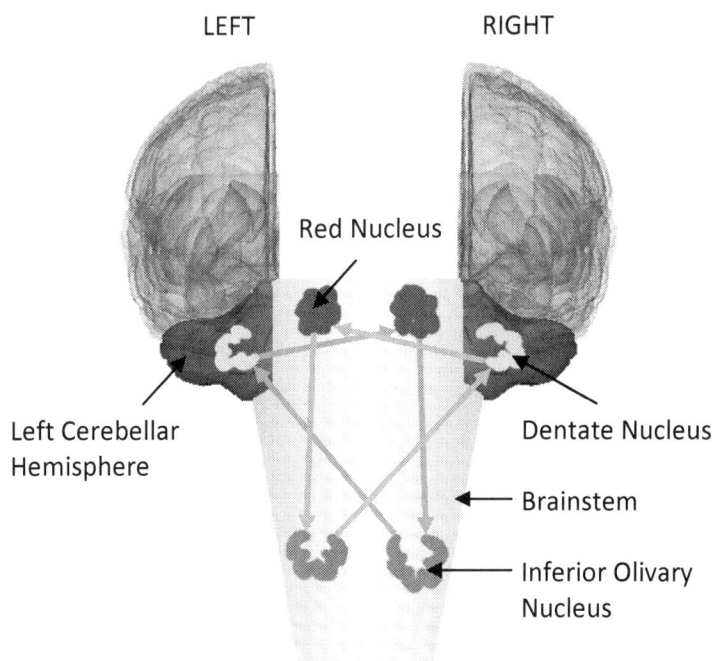

While in the region of the cerebellum it is worthwhile mentioning one of its many functions, which is, error correction. Whenever a motor command is sent from the brain down to the brainstem, a copy of the message is passed to the cerebellum – feed forward – before the command continues to pass down the spinal cord and out along the peripheral nerves to the muscles. Once the motor activity – throwing a dart – is completed, messages pass up the spinal cord to the cerebellum, which then compares what was meant to happen – feed forward – with what did happen – feedback. The cerebellum then sends a message up to the brain saying either "Well done" or if the dart missed the double twenty, suggesting the corrections necessary – up a bit / down a bit. If this system is not functioning as it should, then motor learning can be delayed.

Once we move on to the next stage of play and start using a bat and ball, all manner of things can go wrong. If you struggled to use your hand to catch a ball imagine the problems the brain is going to have when you start using a limb extension. There is a part of the brain that has to know exactly where any part of your body is at any given moment of time and hence when we reach for a cup of tea we don't need to look first to locate our hand because we know where it is and can therefore plan the movement from its starting point. If this area of the brain is not working too well and this may be due to one of the cerebellar hemispheres under-functioning, the use of a bat or racquet which effectively extends the limb by inches, can present computations beyond the scope of the developing brain.

Pencilling in a few details

A term that is tending to crop up more frequently at present is dysgraphia, a posh way to describe difficulties with handwriting. Again, here there tends to be a natural progression starting with the use of crayons for colouring in, followed by coloured pencils before finally getting to grips with a biro or fountain pen. Children that take to colouring-in, drawing and writing often have a vast collection of coloured pencils and pencil cases and may even ask for a really smart fountain pen as a birthday gift. Not so that child that is going to go on to struggle with developing their penmanship. Often these children don't like colouring-in or produce little more than scribble.

An important clue as to what is going on can be gained by observing as early as possible the type of grip the child employs when holding a pencil or crayon. There are two very obvious clues that can be spotted without the need for Dr Watson let alone Sherlock. A fist grip, where the child holds the pencil as if it were a dagger, is saying that in a right-handed child the area on the medial wall of the right side of the brain has not developed as it should. When this happens, fine motor skills are not possible and the function is taken over by another motor area of the brain that unfortunately only knows about the grip that you would require when holding a dagger or spear.

The second clue that the brain is not functioning as it should is when the child employs a clawed grip with exaggerated flexion of both the wrist and elbow. Often this is associated with the use of excessive pressure to the point that the pencil point can break. The cause of this problem is that in the human arm there are more muscles on the front of the limb (palm facing forwards) than on the back and if all the muscles are given the same degree of tone (tension) then rather like a person that has had a stroke, the arm goes into this flexed posture. If the brain is working as it should, then messages should be sent down telling the more powerful and plentiful muscles to ease off a bit and thereby stop overpowering the weaker muscles. This so-called soft pyramidal paresis is a common occurrence in children with dysgraphia and often goes hand in hand with further problems and delays in learning.

The beautiful game???

The transition into becoming a team player is fraught with problems as even at an early age expectations can be high and the less talented player can be excluded or teased about their ineptitude to the point of damaging self esteem and worth. Most people want to be needed, valued and included and no more is this true than with children whose world can end if they are not included within a group of friends in the playground, invited to someone's birthday party or picked for the team. The child that lacks great sporting prowess, struggles to keep pace or is clumsy may suffer from a slow erosion, as opposed to building, of self worth that can have consequences in terms of behaviour, learning and emotional wellbeing.

In an attempt to gain favour a child with dyspraxia or learning difficulties may exaggerate their disability to literally become the joke they see themselves to be or become the class clown, replacing dis-ability with silliness or defiance. As parents it is natural to feel our child's pain when they have taken a tumble and it is second nature to scoop them up and kiss away the tears but how often do we associate the word empathy with the child that is hurting inside but doesn't have the words or indeed the means to tell someone how bad they are feeling. Often because the child cannot explain how they are feeling or they don't want to say what has been happening in their world, the parent is oblivious to their pain and perplexed or angered by their uncharacteristic behaviour.

Being able to pick up on clues and read the signs should be a basic parenting skill but often we are so wrapped up in our own world and with our own worries that we are oblivious to these cries for help or dismiss clear warnings signs as just being naughtiness or a phase they are going through. Recurrent tummy aches, changes in sleeping patterns, a return to bed-wetting or emotional outburst are happening for a reason and it should be part of our job description to respond to them by giving of our time, experience and love. We none of us want to feel that there is anything wrong with our children but when the alarm bells start ringing there is no excuse for being in denial. Things do go wrong for a great many children and rather than burying our heads in the sand we have to realise that the sooner issues are addressed, the sooner they can be fixed.

The signs of stress in children are very much like our own – being edgy, touchy, and even a bit sweaty particularly in the palms of the hands. Being on edge activates an area of the brain that controls our sympathetic nervous system which in turn turns off the digestive system and causes our heart rate to increase. The sympathetic system is designed to be active for only short periods of time while we deal with a threatening event, hence it is often referred to as the fight or flight system. When it is on the verge of firing up over long periods of time, ticking over too fast if you like, then it can cause us in the short-term to be snappy and in the long-term can interfere with our immune system. Recurrent ear infections, constant colds and both eczema and asthma can be signs that the immune system is failing. It may even be the starting point for irritable bowel syndrome, a condition that can plague an individual for a lifetime.

Actions speak louder

After dyspraxia, problems with attention and/or levels of activity are the most common symptom of behavioural or learning disabilities to follow. Whereas the signs and symptoms of dyspraxia can be missed or overlooked, attention deficits and hyperactivity can drive parents to despair. However, if as parents we are going to really understand just what is going on in any child's head we have to be able to differentiate between what is 'normal' behaviour for a child of a particular age and what may prove to be an invaluable sign that things are not progressing quite as they should. If you expect your ten year old child to listen to your request to fetch your slippers when they are running upstairs their mind buzzing with all that they are going to have to do to get to the next level of whatever computer game they have just paused, you are living in cuckoo land. It is no different to a female of the species waxing lyrical about the benefits of a new designer handbag while the male of the species is listening to the football results. It is just not going to happen.

There is a subtle and yet very important difference between simply not listening because you have other more important things on your mind, attention deficit and a poor memory. Most young children will remember simple instructions that are whispered in their ear, while they do not register the request that is shouted up the stairs. It is all about focus and priorities in a young mind. If you are really concerned that your child may have real issues next time you ask them to bring your slippers down for you add "….. and by the way there is a five pound note for you on the dressing table". If that doesn't work you may have a problem or your child might have a hearing problem. Many children that have had recurrent ear infections have reduced hearing and every now and then a child slips through the net and is actually deaf. If in doubt see your GP.

Distractibility in children is a universal complaint driven by the amazing array of stimuli that are going on around them and the reduced ability in young children to filter out trivial stimuli. The primitive reflexes that cause us to look at anything that moves in our immediate environment or the need to locate the source of a sound need to be attenuated so that we can focus on what is really important while filtering out everything else that is not important to the task in hand or an immediate threat. There is a fine dividing line between this immature infantile lack of sensory input filtering and the adult mature state. How many of us have become all too aware that our clothes are irritating us or the humming of the air-con unit is getting on our nerves when we are overtired or bored?

To become truly focused we must firstly become grounded. That is, to be in touch with whatever we are standing upon and be confident of our balance and security. This is principally a function of the cerebellum and the starting point of all that is to follow. Next we need to be spatially aware. This means we have to master our primitive reflexes and be able visually to focus with our eyes and the non-seeing areas of our visual system on what is important. Seeing is said to be believing but this is one of, if not, the biggest, falsehoods in nature. We only see what we want to see or need to see. Interest and survival drives vision – what we see – the rest remains unconscious until it reaches critical levels. Subconscious seeing monitors such things as light levels – the coming of dusk – what is happening around us – potential threats – and where we are relative to our immediate environment – our position in space.

Spatial awareness is critical to survival and yet is missing in both Mr Bean and many children. To be spatially aware we must know where we are relative to our immediate surroundings and maintain subconscious vigilance and relevance to change, whilst focusing upon our chosen task. The ability to accomplish such tasks relies upon the 'Where" part of the visual system that resides in the parietal cortex – an area of the cortex towards the back that processes a wide variety of sensory stimuli – and an area of the medial wall at the very back, that processes and monitors our every movement so we know where each part of our body is at any one moment. As this area of the brain is fed by information from our muscles and joints, principally via the cerebellum, any malfunctions downstream can cause major problems. No wonder Mr Bean and so many children have problems.

Lastly, we have to maintain 'mental' focus, that is, while doing everything we need to do physically to maintain our balance and posture, and while monitoring our surroundings, still remain focused on our chosen task. This is a function of our prefrontal cortex and the anterior cingulated, the very front of the medial wall, plays a crucial role in this. If the anterior cingulated under-functions it is impossible to keep still, resist impulses, remain focused and to have an effective working memory. No surprise then that varying degrees of malfunction here can be the cause of attention deficit, fidgeting, impulsive acts or full-blown hyperactivity.

In children the lack of focus can impact upon learning and the inability to keep still and resist the temptation to blurt out an answer can disrupt a class and make teaching a nightmare. But it is not just children that suffer from attention deficit and hyperactivity, as ADD and ADHD are not self-limiting conditions that come to an end – as was once thought – with the onset of puberty. The idea that ADHD would eventually burn itself out was perhaps the reasoning behind the use of stimulant medication, to keep the child under control until nature took over. As stimulant medication only masks the symptoms of ADHD, it is not a cure and is not without its side-effects, it would seem wise to look for a drug free treatment that would address the cause and not just make life easier for those people caring for the sufferer.

Untreated full-blown ADHD can be carried over into adult life with dire consequences. It has been linked to oppositional defiant disorder (ODD) characterised by disobedience, aggressive and defiant behaviour directed towards adults that falls short of actual physical violence. However, it has been reported that more than 50% of children with ODD will develop a conduct disorder that may include criminal activities and actual physical assaults. It has been suggested that children with ADHD may have an addictive personality initially manifested by a craving for sugar and later a raised probability of smoking, heavy drinking and the use of drugs. It has been said that more than 70% of male inmates in young offender institutions have the criteria for a diagnosis of ADHD.

Sub-clinical ADHD can pass unnoticed into adulthood. Often the child is said to be just being a boy or described as a lively character but in adulthood the sub-clinical signs can impact upon every aspect of life. As everything and I do mean everything has to be done in a rush, food is bolted, work completed without due care and a swift pint or more likely pints is taken literally. The sub-clinical adult cannot keep still, is always on the go and is incapable of slowing down and enjoying the moment.

Ding dong

Just as a sugar craving in a young child may be an early warning sign of troubles ahead, so delays in reaching milestones, evidence of dyspraxia and attentional issues may be a forewarning of troubles ahead when the child starts school and formal learning and/or the development of tics or obsessive traits. However, as the brain continues to grow through infancy and on into adolescence, the correct interventions at the earliest possible stage can help prevent not only the child from suffering unnecessarily but also reduce considerably the need for parental strategies and premature hair loss.

FURTHER CLUES

Clumsy
Messy eater
Late developer
Accident prone
Late riding a bike
Problems dressing
Not good at sports
Poor attention / hyper
Poor spatial awareness
Poor handwriting / grip
Mixed dominance hand / eye /foot

5 THE WORLD OUTSIDE

All the world's a stage

Apart from days out with mum and the odd get together with the other mums and their offspring that were in the maternity unit at the same time, formal playgroups or nursery school can be the first time a child gets to mix with other children and be left by their mother. For children of working mums the wrench may be reduced somewhat by having already been left with a nanny, au pair or childminder but for many being separated from mum can be too much to bear. Usually it is the parent that suffers most when the screaming child is left in the capable arms of the nursery teacher or assistant but for some children being left by mum is a traumatic event. It is perfectly normal for a child to be upset when mum disappears for a while but for a small percentage of children it generates real separation anxiety. Here the child cannot be comforted or distracted and remains very distressed until mum returns. Over time the apparent level of distress may lessen but this is often because the child is withdrawing into themselves as a means of coping.

Possible signs of anxiety in young children:

- Excessive crying or whining
- Clinginess – constantly wanting to be held
- Hiding behind parent - holding hand or leg
- Shyness – other than initially
- Silence – becoming withdrawn
- Not mixing with other children

It is a prime function of the right side of the brain to deal with any new situation and following a quick appraisal decide whether to remain or withdraw. If for any reason the right side of the brain is not developing as it should, then new situations are avoided and if they are unavoidable the immediate response is distress. The brain of a toddler is not only growing but does not contain the full compliment of second generation neurons that must form, migrate to specific areas of the prefrontal cortex and very importantly start to function. This window of development has been called bpoptosis and any delays in this process can underlie learning and behavioural issues in children.

Adult v child's brain

You reading *this* word, that is, the fully processed realisation of a precise moment of time has been called the global emotional moment. To achieve it every single event going on inside your body has to be monitored, processed repeatedly at different levels of your nervous system before being brought to a tiny area of the brain called the insular in the prefrontal cortex. While this is going on, in exactly the same time frame, all the sensory information coming into your body has to be filtered and repeatedly processed before being blended with all the processed information about how your body is functioning. Once this is done the sum of the internal and external data is moved forward to the middle area of the insular where all the processed emotional data is added. Only when this has happened can the final product of all this processing be passed forward to the anterior insular to create the global emotional moment you experienced when reading *this*.

With every global emotional moment there comes an opportunity to decide upon a response that will be coloured by the constituents of that moment. The child does not have the full compliment of brain cells let alone the ability or indeed experience to process information at an adult level and hence the way their brain functions is at a more primitive level and hence their responses to situations can be very different. All the while the child's brain is under-functioning due purely to its immaturity, the child relies upon its parents to make right brain decisions and provide the feeling of security every child needs. Knowing this empowers the parent and realising that so many of the functions we take for granted, for instance time, do not exist in the child's brain, helps to provide a reason behind the tantrum that follows anything that involves delayed gratification.

Playing for time

Playing, initially alone and later with others, enables us to develop a vast range of bodily skills which will be encoded into movement patterns which in turn will make it easier to learn further more advanced skills. It is also the beginnings of developing a raft of social skills necessary to live and survive in a complex society and the starting point of learning. The basics of social skills involve meeting, greeting and engaging with others and the starting point is learning how to physically handle a new potential playmate. Too in-your-face or too physically rough and it's going to end in tears, while being too timid is going to greatly hinder progress. The child that is a whirlwind and as a result constantly ends up hurting other children will be avoided by other children and parents alike. The child that is too active or the child that gets overexcited all too easily and we have all seen them at birthday parties, should be telling you his - and yes it is usually going to be a boy - diet needs close attention and immediate changes making to it.

The child that is excessively shy, hides behind you or the furniture when anyone arrives, avoids eye contact and won't speak may be showing signs of a developmental delay or if in combination with other signs autistic traits. There are subtle and yet crucially important differences between autistic traits and real autism and these need to be evaluated and addressed at an early age. Often in the nursery situation the child that is struggling does not join in with the other children but prefers to remain on the periphery either playing alone or watching the other children playing with a series of furtive glances. The child in such a situation cannot understand their plight but from a safe distance can try to work out what they are meant to do in this strange environment and without their ever present mother.

Who is hurting?

The child that is aggressive towards other children on a regular basis is either unaware of their physical strength, may be lacking in guidance from their parents or may be hurting themselves. That is, the child may not have the experience of how to interact with other children and the new parent how to deal with situations when they start to go wrong. Also, the child that is not guided and rewarded for good behaviour may face constant frustrations and negative adult responses which can lead to outwardly aggressive acts. Much of what a child learns early on is based on copying the behaviour of family members. An older brother with hyperactivity is not a good role model and physical evidence of a marital breakdown is going to leave a young brain very confused as to what is right or wrong.

Imagine that

Imaginary play is an important learning stage for children helping them to not only learn new physical skills but also to engage in such activities as planning, the development of ideas and even lateral thinking. It is a natural tendency of children to mimic the activities of their parents and the amazing collection of mini cooking stoves and tools in any toyshop bears witness to this. However, it is the child's ability to create their own imaginary kitchen or workshop out of cardboard boxes that is a sure sign that their brain is developing as it should but even at this early stage, showing signs of creativity. The child that cannot play independently, needs to be guided or led, may be showing signs of developmental delay.

When parents discover that their child has an imaginary friend it is often a cause for concern. Is it a bad thing and does it mean that something is wrong or lacking in the child's life? The consensus of opinion is that it is not a problem and may in fact help the child to develop a host of essential skills including communication and social interaction. They can provide companionship to an only child and a comfort to any child in times of stress. They are also someone to boss around and someone to take the blame for anything that gets broken. It is not unusual to hear a child chattering away, when on their own in the playroom and this is a good time to do a little eavesdropping just to make sure everything is OK. A child that is being bullied or is worried about something may talk it over with their imaginary friend when they are unable to tell a parent.

Imaginary friends may appear to be very real, can be described in great detail and like real friends have their likes and dislikes but ultimately do not really exist in the child's mind. However, this perfect friendship can be put to effective use by a parent that asks the friend for an opinion or praises the friend for eating all their greens. An imaginary friend should be welcomed into the family, should not be a cause for ridicule by older siblings and should be appreciated for the confidence and learning potential they can give a child.

Gaining control

No matter how the family unit is constructed – nuclear, extended, single parent – the chances are that there will be input from the in-laws / out-laws and although this can be well meant and valuable, it may also cause friction and leave a new parent not knowing what to do for the best. With a nuclear family it may be 'His' mother putting her oar in directly as in "We never did it that way in my day" or even worse when 'He' says "My mother thinks you are not feeding him enough and that's why he is always crying". The old-fashion truly extended family where everybody lives virtually on the doorstep has many advantages providing that the family accepts you and you literally marry into the family. The single parent's situation may be complicated by their personal history and any baggage that has been carried forward, together with financial implications and having to physically and mentally cope alone.

The arrival of the first-born is usually a time of great joy but once the infant is established in the home his/her presence can provide a number of unexpected interruptions to the well established patterns of daily and nightly activities. Apart from the sleepless nights that inevitably happen, there is also the need to establish new routines centred about the infant's needs and a loss of the spontaneous night out that was previously an option. The new division of labour can also become a source of irritation where the new mum feels she is doing more than her fair share and sometimes the new dad feels that being the wage-earner is his full-time job and that childcare is not really in his job description. Nightly visits to the pub, the boys' night out on Fridays and football on Saturday, once tolerated in the past can now put strain on a relationship when the housebound mother can feel she is missing out.

Parents and grandparents can be a great asset in the new situation the couple find themselves in and can help considerably in the sudden transition from care free couple into responsible parents. By providing moral support, advice, baby-sitting and financial assistance if required or gifted, the family members from both sides can make the new parents lives more comfortable and afford them many opportunities to be more efficient and effective in their new roles. There is no formal training for parenthood and unfortunately bad role models can imprint upon impressionable minds habits, routines and behavioural that is not desirable or acceptable. This can range from eating habits that rely upon take-a-ways and junk food, to poor hygiene standards or moral standards that contravene the laws of society.

The new family has the opportunity because it is new to retain the very best of the old, while rejecting old bad habits and setting new standards. This may well require seeking help from a favourite aunt or simply taking a greater interest in home cooking or it may need a great deal or tact and diplomacy to get across to your partner, friends or family that swearing, passing wind in public, smoking dope, shoplifting, etc., are not acceptable forms of behaviour. Without taking the moral high ground it is essential to get across to any significant person in a child's life that their actions will direct the course of your child's future and that you have a moral obligation to decide just what you want your child to consider normal actions, reactions and behaviour.

Losing control

Once you hand over the care and control of your child to a third party a number of potential issues may arise. This may be grandparents providing huge quantities of brightly coloured sweets, a baby-sitter more interested in texting friends than in attending to your child's safety or the rigid regime at the local nursery school. Sometimes a little detective work is required before the reasons behind your child's behaviour, hyperactivity or mood change on returning from a day out with grandparents can be explained. If, as is often the case, it is due to a cocktail of fizzy drinks and sweets, they must be told kindly but in no uncertain terms that it must not happen in the future. Parents and grandparents will often provide such 'treats' on the excuse that you are only young once but in buying the child's affection, they are potentially damaging your relationship with your child if you have to bear the brunt of chemically driven explosive behaviour later in the day.

Of all the everyday things that can be a problem, what others feed your child/children is perhaps the most common. Anyone that doubts that there is a link between what you feed a child and their behaviour only needs to watch TV the next time there is a programme that involves an expert – Super Nanny or Tanya Byron – being called in to deal with the child from hell. Note what exactly the child (and parents) are eating and drinking, where meals take place and how they are consumed. Also, whenever possible note what other little goodies are on the kitchen work surfaces or lurking in the cupboards. A diet based on carbohydrates, bad fats, crisps, sweets, squashes and fizzy drinks does not make for a quiet life and is probably causing, if not driving, the behaviour of the child from hell.

Realising the link is one thing but avoiding it is not always that easy even though in theory it should be. Within the confines of your own home you can decide on what and where your child eats but at nursery, in school or when visiting friends things can be beyond your control and as Jamie Oliver found to his cost, an uphill struggle. The problem is, that once some children get a taste for sweets, fizzy drinks and junk food they will not only demand them constantly but when refused will beg, borrow or steal to get them. The child that has developed a taste if not addiction to such foods and beverages will swop the contents of his lunch box, trade toys or even help himself from mum's purse to feed the need.

With Christmas, Easter, birthdays and holidays, it seems as though there is always a reason why a child has to have sweets, treats, chocolate and junk food in excessive quantities. Even for the parents that provide an excellent well balanced home cooked diet for their child, there seems to be an over-riding desire, almost a guilt that drives them to go off the rails and for the parents that feel that a good diet is not important; this is a time to really pig-out. If your child had a severe nut allergy or diabetes, would you say "Come on, it's Christmas, let him have some nuts" or "It's his birthday, surely he can have one day off!" All things in moderation should be a motto for life and therefore a treat should be a treat and not an expected multi-daily occurrence. A glass of wine might just settle the nerves and provide that little bit of Dutch courage needed to chat-up the girl of your dreams, while getting totally paralytic might just ruin any chance you had.

As there is little doubt that food additives can cause immediate and sometimes long lasting effects in some children and the chances are that all children would be better off without them, it is necessary to be diplomatic but firm with family members and to make a point of finding out what your child is to be fed when at school, in after school club or at scouts' camp. This may seem like taking things too far but as you are what you eat, healthy eating should not be something that is subject to compromise and dropped for the sake of an easy life. If you are Jewish, Muslim or if your child has a severe nut allergy your food and that provided for your child must be kosher, halal or nut free and feeble excuses such as not knowing what the childminder provides would not excuse a bacon sandwich or a bar of hazelnut chocolate.

Parenting at its most basic level is all about promoting the survival of the child. To achieve this we provide food and drink, shelter, warmth, cleanliness, clothes, physical contact and love. To this we add play, learning what is right and wrong, avoiding danger, learning by example and then formal education. All children must be safe, happy and be given every opportunity to reach their potential in life. To attain this end every aspect of their physical and emotional needs must be attended to with both care and attention to detail. Knowing how the brain grows, develops, functions and malfunctions can greatly assist a parent in not only understanding the developmental stages all children pass through but will help in making the right decisions with regard to such basics as diet and discipline even when everything is fine, to what next when things have gone horribly wrong.

CASE HISTORY 2 – The Smith family

Mrs. Smith was not a happy lady. She had brought her two sons to the clinic to be assessed and by the time they left I too had all but lost the will to live. Both the boys had a typical history of birth trauma/foetal distress, delays in attaining their developmental milestones, hyperactivity and under-achievement at school. On examination both showed signs of under-functioning of the left cerebellum and the right cortex. When their eye movements were assessed using a computer generated test, they both demonstrated abnormal pursuits (slow movements), saccades (fast movements) and convergence failure.

I sent them away with a diet sheet, a list of supplements to be taken daily and a couple of balancing exercises to be perfected. When seen some six weeks later their diet was still a nutritionist's nightmare, the supplements had not been taken and clearly the exercises had not even been attempted let alone perfected. Clearly the frustration and disappointment I felt must have shown on my face. Mrs. Smith, now close to tears, instead of spouting a torrent of excuses I was expecting, simply said she could not cope. Her husband had gone off two years ago since when things had gone from bad to worse. Fortunately for me, at this point Mrs. Smith started talking about her childhood and asked me if I would consider seeing her for an assessment.

Mrs. Smith's case history and examination results were almost identical to the boys. She had been born by emergency Caesarean section due to foetal distress, was late attaining most of her developmental milestones and at school had struggled to learn to read, hated spelling tests and had the attention span of a gnat. She had been in constant trouble at school and at home due to her inability to organize anything or remain focused for more than a millisecond.

What I needed here was commitment. If I was going to be able to do anything at all to help Mrs. Smith, let alone the boys, she was going to have to follow the treatment regime to the letter. The starting point had to be the diet and supplements. Currently, they were all eating a diet based on processed foods laced with fizzy drinks. While carbs ruled, fruit and veg figured nowhere in this recipe for disaster and Mrs. Smith alone could down approaching two litres of a well known fizzy drink a day.

Away she went again, this time promising to stick to the diet, buy fresh fruit and veg and start cooking from scratch. I cannot say I was in the least bit confident of the outcome, but I can but try. When seen again two months later, the boys were calm and actually managed to sit still during the entire consultation, while Mrs. Smith had a smile a mile wide. The diet was in place, the supplements were being taken and the exercises had become a matter of personal pride. Obviously the boys were better but the change in their mother was quite remarkable. She said that it was like the haze had cleared and she could now see and not only was she calmer but for the first time in her life she felt in control.

Over a period of several months the Smiths took on new exercises, computer generated treatment for their convergence failure and other programs designed to stimulate the right side of their brains. The boys remained calm and I have to say a pleasure to be with but also had started to achieve at school. Mrs. Smith apparently met Mr. Right and when last seen in clinic was a different woman.

CASE HISTORY 3 – Ronan age 7

By the time Ronan attempted to enter the world he already had three sisters and two brothers and was set to live an idyllic life on a farm in Co. Cork, Ireland. I say attempted as the very active feotus as he was then had somehow managed to get the umbilical cord not once, but twice, around his neck. This caused him great distress as he tried unsuccessfully to leave the womb and his mother and midwife a few very scary minutes.

Ronan attained all his developments milestones without a glitch and from the moment he learnt to crawl was into everything. Once he learnt how to defy gravity and master the art of walking and in no time at all running, the farm became his own personal playground. From the minute he awoke to the time late in the evening when eventually he succumbed to exhaustion, he was a whirlwind that only ever stopped to eat and even then could not sit still for a second.

Initially school was a welcome extention to places he could explore and activities he could engage in, but any plans for him to sit and listen, let alone learn, were simply not going to happen. The physical limitations of the playground could just about be tolerated but the confines of the classroom and the need to keep still for periods of time were an impossibility. Ronan excelled at sport and was very popular with the other children but his constant running around, shouting out and as a consequence, inability to learn, was wearing very thin with his teachers.

In clinic Ronan struggled to keep still for five minutes which made the consultation and examination something of an exercise in patience and persistence. What was clear was that Ronan's diet was fueling his hyperactivity and needed to be addressed before considering anything else. Therefore, I sent Ronan and his mother away with a simple diet sheet and list of supplements for him to take on a daily basis.

When seen some two months later the supplementation and diet were in place but Ronan was as active as ever, showing no real sign of improvement at all. I talked to his mother about the diet and supplementation and I have to say it was faultless. For a moment I was baffled until Ronan chipped in and provided the vital piece of evidence that had been missing until that point. While his mother and the school were keeping a very close eye on his dietary in take, his grandmother was spending 40 euros a week on sweets and doughnuts for the children, and guess who was taking the lions share?

Two months later I saw Ronan again. This time he was able to sit relatively still, complete the tests I needed to carry out and start the next phase of the treatment. It was never going to be easy, with temptation lying around ever corner but over the next few months Ronan became calmer, stuck to the diet and started to learn. His grandmother who had to spoil the grandchildren was eventually persuaded to spend her euros on books and games.

6 THE LEARNING CURVE

Although all learning starts with play, the imitation of others and our interaction with others there are many subtle factors that unknowingly can influence our ability to learn. It has been suggested that listening to classical music while still in the womb can have positive effects upon the development of the foetal brain and many years ago it was said that the number of books in the home could be used as a predictive factor of a child's academic success. More recently it has been stated that the number of stories a child listens to while sat on a parents or grandparent lap while looking at the colourful pictures can have a powerful effect on the child's ability to learn to read.

How we are taught, what we are taught and where we are taught will influence the rate at which we learn but also how the brain is developing or not may help or hinder our advances in learning and the very subject matter will necessitate the development and usage of different patterns of brain function. Before the advent of the written word, knowledge was passed on via the spoken word and required the development of a very good memory. Once alphabets had been created and the written word became more commonplace, the memory could be left to rest between the pages of a book until needing to be recalled. Socrates feared that much would be lost if the oral tradition with the natural flexibility it contained were to be replaced with the literally 'written in stone' use of the written word. Similar fears have been aired concerning our current move into the digital world, with emails and texting corrupting and limiting the more aesthetic qualities of language. A joke told well by someone who can mimic an accent, imitate the actions and get the timing right might just contain something more than the written word and certainly outstrips the often vulgar texts that rely heavily upon obscenity and very little political correctness.

ORAL v WRITTEN v TEXTING WORDS OF LOVE	
Oral:	Holding her hands adds physicality before the words "I love you, I want you" are carried on warm breath to caress the waiting ear.
Written:	It takes a little more with just words to bring to life your true feeling – A hesitant first touch bridges the abyss between watching and wanting and slight fingers guide such appetite to her mouth, that frightened of bruising the kiss, trembles in anticipation and desiring all things that the kiss holds promise to, blends loves and lives in a tribute to nature. I love you.
Text:	Bbz fink ur reli gorjuz n luv ya loadz. Wanna be wiv u 4eva. Fink ur amazing, dnt wanna lose u, luvs ya xxx

In Jordan most children learn to read and write in both English and Arabic. Many children with learning disabilities find it harder to learn to read and write in Arabic and although continuing to speak Arabic as their first language drop reading and writing in Arabic in favour of English. To write in Arabic necessitates using a cursive and fairly complicated script to be used right from the start, whereas in English we learn to write the individual letters of the alphabet before joining them up. Also, although many children who struggle to learn to read have an increased number of regressions – the eyes moving right to left – it would appear that it is easier for the brain to drive the eyes left to right when reading.

English:

In Arabic we both read and write from right to left.

Arabic:

اليســــار الــى اليميــــن من العربيـــــة اللغــة نقــرأ نحــن

To write in Chinese requires the mastery of the 2,000 characters of the alphabet which is usually achieved by 10-11 years of age. This remarkable feat is made possible by using the visual areas of the brain on both sides, whereas for English and Japanese only the left visual area is used. This is a very good example of how adaptable the human brain is, being able to utilise extra storage as required but also serves to illustrate how a background knowledge of neurology can be put to use to explain to parents difficulties that a child may be experiencing in learning to read or write.

To write in any language requires great manual dexterity and this is usually achieved in a gradual process starting with scribbling, then drawing and then learning to write. Most people are right-handed and in order to pass from a fist grip and start using the fingers, necessitates the development and maturation of the motor fields of the right brain including the medial wall. As developmental delay of the right side of the brain is usually the underlying cause of most of the learning and behavioural disorders, it is no surprise that a high percentage of children have a poor pen grip, struggle to write well and often complain of the arm aching after a few short sentences.

Many young children fail to stay on task and seem to be distracted by anything that is going on around them. This is often interpreted as being attention deficit, that is, the mental inability to remain focused - a prime function of the anterior cingulate area of the medial wall. However, recent research would suggest that many young children have a retained primitive defensive visual reflex which causes them to direct their central vision towards anything that appears in their peripheral visual fields. It is a function of the right parietal cortex – towards the back of the brain – to monitor what is going on around us but we must be able to suppress the desire to look at objects that appear or move unless there is a real threat to us.

It has been suggested that more than 30% of children that struggle to learn to read and may be considered as having dyslexia, have in fact a problem in bringing their eyes in towards the nose, which is essential for all close work. As convergence insufficiency can be diagnosed in minutes and treated in weeks in the vast majority of cases, it is something that every parent, teacher and optician should be aware of. If you or your child have been tested for convergence you are in a very small minority. Convergence is the ability to bring both eyes in towards the nose at the same time and with the same degree of accuracy. The target, whatever we are looking at, has to be projected onto the retina of each eye very accurately for the brain to be able to accept and process the information effectively. If one eye, and it is usually the left, does not come into convergence with sufficient accuracy, the brain has to suppress the information it provides or suffer double-vision.

Accurate convergence is not only essential for effective close vision but is also an important precursor to smooth tracking and reading fluency. It is possible to see exactly what a child's eyes are doing as they read a short passage by the use of a computer generated test called a Visagraph. The test which takes just a couple of minutes involves the child wearing some goggles that contain movement sensors while reading a short passage. The recorded eye movements are passed to a computer that analyses the individual eye movements from each eye and produces a report including the number of times each eye stopped and regressed (moved right to left). It then very cleverly superimposes the combined eye movements over the passage that has just been read. With poor readers it is not unusual to have ten times the number of stops and regressions. No wonder the child struggles to read and finds no pleasure in it.

> **THE MOST COMMON SYMPTOMS ASSOCIATED WITH CONVERGENCE INSUFFICIENCY**
>
> Eyestrain – often associated with tearing
>
> Headache – often around the eyes
>
> Double vision
>
> Blurred vision
>
> Words appearing to move on the page
>
> Slow reading speed
>
> Poor concentration

It has been said that when ignorance is bliss it is folly to be wise but how would a child feel and react if they were indeed wise and yet struggle to read, get spellings, write and grasp the basics of number skills? The answer is that often these children become the class clown or at home vent their frustrations in angry outbursts. The child with convergence insufficiency does not know they have a visual problem that is making it harder for them to read than their peers but what they do know is that they must be stupid because they are struggling and added to this being taken out of class for extra help can often serve to confirm that they are rubbish. All children should be safe, happy and able to reach their full potential in life. Once a child realises that they are not keeping up with their peers, their self esteem can take a real knock and the joy of just being alive can be lost.

Long before a child's confidence, self worth and self esteem hits rock bottom, it is necessary to pick up on any warning signs and act upon them immediately. Any change in behaviour should be noted and any feedback from school, whether just a word from a teacher, end of term report or from a parents' evening may require a good deal of thought if not action. Any suggestion of bullying requires instant firm action to ensure it is dealt with immediately and stamped out. If the school seem reluctant to act immediately to resolve the situation, take it to the next level without further ado. Persistent bullying for whatever reason can leave a child's ego scarred and can cause long-term damage to the adolescent.

As love conquers all, you do not need to be a top notch detective to pick up the clues early on that things may not be quite right in your child's little world. Just by watching and listening it is relatively easy to piece together what might be going on and then it is just a matter of finding the right moment to gently broach the issue. When doing this it is important to tell the child how much you love them, how fantastic they are and how proud you are of them, so that they may find the confidence within the loving relationship to share with you something that is very difficult for them to share. Sometimes this approach only meets with anger and resentment, which is all the more reason to delve deeper, perhaps by other means to find the underlying cause.

CASE HISTORY 4 – sudden onset bed-wetting

John, now aged eight, entered the world without a problem, was breast fed and reached each milestone on time with the exception of crawling and gaining nocturnal continence until nearly seven. Once at school he took to reading like a duck to water, had no problems with his spellings and excelled at maths. The feedback from school could not have been better and it was said that he was the model pupil. He did not like sport, wasn't much good at it and had told his mother he had two left feet.

One morning during the autumn term Mary, his mother, discovered that he had wet the bed. When he came home from school she tried to have a quiet word with him about it but her usually happy, loving son, erupted like a volcano. He lashed out, screamed at her and ran off upstairs to his room. Shocked, hurt and angry, she tried to work out in her mind what was happening and what could have caused such a reaction, before sitting down and bursting into tears. John did not come down when he was called and not wanting to face another upset, left his meal on the table. When she went upstairs later John was in bed fast asleep.

In the morning there was silence and another wet bed. Mary did not say anything to John about it and dropped him off at school as usual. Once he was inside the school gates she drove off but instead of heading off for work, parked up around the corner from where she would have a clear view of the playground. Had anyone asked her what she was doing there staring at the playground, she would have struggled to find an answer but not for long. Within a couple of minutes she saw two boys that appeared to be twice the size of John roughing him up. They pushed him around threw his books across the playground and tipped the contents of his lunchbox on the ground and trod on it. Laughing, they left their dishevelled victim to collect his books.

More tears welled up in Mary's eyes as she watched her son, head bent in shame, walk off leaving his lunch for the pigeons. The tears did not last for long and were quickly replaced by a response you would expect from a lioness seeing her cubs in danger. By the time Mary had left the Head's office he would have been in no doubt about the lack of supervision in the playground that morning and that bullying cannot be tolerated. The wet beds continued for another couple of nights before all returned to normal.

CASE HISTORY 5 – live wire

Darren, aged six, was reluctant to enter the world and only made the move with the assistance of some rather large forceps. He was breast fed, was a little delayed on reaching his developmental milestones and was a complete joy to his mother until he started walking. From that point on he was constantly on the move from the crack of dawn until, exhausted, he went to bed. At playschool it was noted he was a very lively child and several times it had been necessary for interventions to be put in place due to his boisterous behaviour. In Reception, things had gone from bad to worse, with Darren being totally unable to sit still for a minute, being totally disruptive and even with the guidance of a classroom assistant being impossible to engage in any activity that might lead to learning.

When seen in clinic, Darren was on the move continually and without supervision would have left a trail of destruction behind him. However, as the consultation and examination continued it became very evident that something was driving this supercharged behaviour and that was his diet. From an early age Darren had directed his diet and now virtually dictated what he would eat and when he would eat. At that time Darren had three main meals, four snacks, sometimes an additional supper and continuous sweets, all of which had to be washed down with a well known fizzy drink.

By the time Darren left the clinic he was not a very happy chap, had said a couple of very rude words and had told his parents in no uncertain terms that the dietary changes suggested were not going to happen.

	Suggested supplements – Vegepa (Omega 3-6), Kindervital (vitamins) and Floradix saludynam (minerals)	
	Old Diet	**New Diet**
Breakfast	Sugar coated cereal	Cooked breakfast (scrambled egg etc.)
Snacks	Crisps, biscuits, cakes, sweets	Apple
Lunch	Jam sandwiches, crisps, chocolate, cakes, sweets	Ham/cheese sandwich, carrot sticks, fruit
Snacks	Cakes, biscuits, crisps, sweets	Chopped vegetables with dips, fruit
Dinner	Pasta or pizza with chips	Home cooked meal
Supper	Cereals or sandwich, sweet	

Fortunately, Darren's parents had followed the suggested dietary changes to the letter and after what was described as a living hell for two weeks; Darren had suddenly accepted the changes and became a very different young man. When seen in clinic eight weeks later he was calm, did as he was asked and remarkably his parents had received a glowing report from the school regarding behaviour in class.

A great many children if allowed will dictate what they will eat and perhaps with the power of advertising will be drawn towards a diet of carbohydrates and processed foods often laden with sugar, salt, bad e numbers and artificial sweeteners. As to a certain extent we are what we eat, the dietary equivalent of rocket fuel is not going to make for a peaceful life.

CASE HISTORY 6 – a minor distraction

Millie, aged six, made the perfect entrance into the world, arrived promptly at all her milestones and had no problems letting go of her mother's apron strings and settling into nursery school. However, once in Reception it became apparent that although Millie could sit fairly still, she was unable to complete any task given to her as she was constantly distracted by everything and anything going on around her.

It had been suggested that she might be suffering from attention deficit disorder and that perhaps she needed to see someone. What became very apparent during the consultation was that there seemed to be two Millie's, one that could play happily in her room, whether it be drawing or arranging her doll's house, the other that could not focus on the job in hand for more than two seconds.

On examination, Millie struggled to both bring her eyes into convergence and to remain looking at the target for more than a second and she also could not resist the temptation to look at a moving object during visual field testing even though constantly asked to stare at an object in front of her. It was clear that in her room where nothing moved she could concentrate and remain focused on her drawing or whatever, whereas in the busy classroom she was a martyr to a primitive visual reflex.

Using computer generated treatment programmes it was possible to address Millie's convergence issue within four months and suppress the visual reflex shortly afterwards. Convergence insufficiency is a common problem in children with both learning and behavioural issues and is a significant factor in more than 30% of children. The retention of a primitive defensive visual reflex is also something that should be considered when a young child seems incapable of keeping their eyes on the job in front of them.

CASE HISTORY 7 – can't see for looking

Mark, aged eight, entered the world with the help of a Ventouse assisted delivery. He was slightly delayed in reaching all his milestones and once in Reception struggled to read and when writing often reversed both letters and numbers. His maths was described as being very good.

When talking to Mark during the consultation he came across as a very bright young man, with well developed social skills and a great sense of humour. As with so many children seen in clinic, clearly something was right here, as this obviously very bright, highly articulate young man had a reading age of six years. Once the examination was underway the cause of his problems became all too evident. When tested for convergence both manually and by using a computer generated test he demonstrated convergence failure. Not only did he struggle to bring his eyes in towards his nose accurately but the left eye failed to remain in convergence quickly moving back to the central position.

Further testing using a Visagraph demonstrated to Mark and his parents just why this bright young man could not read. The number of times his right eye stopped while reading the short passage was ten times more than it should have been (1024) but even more significantly his left eye stopped more than 12 times more than it should (1284). The number of regressions – eyes moving right to left – were also 10/12 more than they should have been. Put simply, the two eyes were not moving in sync and nearly 50% of the time he was reading backwards. Imagine the confusion this must cause when WAS becomes SAW and b and d become interchangeable.

As Mark and his parents watched the Visagraph simulation they all shed a tear. Mark because now he knew there was a physical reason behind his inability to read and his parents probably due to a strange mixture of guilt and relief. Six months on and Mark was reading fluently with a reading age slightly above his eight years and as said when he was seen last "You will never look back".

FURTHER CLUES

Late speech development
Continued use of the fist-grip
Poor at colouring-in
Clawed or flexed pen grip
Poor handwriting
Aching hand/arm when writing
Struggles with reading
Have signs of convergence problem
Poor spelling
Struggles with basic number skills

7 ENGLAND EXPECTS

We want the best for our children and therefore expect the best from them but unfortunately sometimes they can't always deliver the behaviour we expect, or academically live up to our expectations. With a greater knowledge of how their brain should grow and develop it may be possible to gain a better understanding into what we should expect, taking into account the variations that will be unique to each child and to know why glitches occur and what to do about them. Let's face it, if every child was perfect in every way and life was idyllic there would be no need for these words and job centres would be full of educational psychologists looking for work.

As it stands, none of us receive a formal education in parenting and even if we did, it surely would not prepare us for all the slings-and-arrows that life can throw at us. Losing your spouse, facing financial ruin, discovering that your child has autism or that your teenage son is taking drugs can take you to breaking point regardless of your social standing or faith. As none of us are immortal, few immune to recessions and in ever increasing numbers we are having to face up to learning and behavioural issues in our children, it is essential to gain the greatest possible insight into what goes on inside the mind of an infant, child and adolescent.

Growth factors

Twenty years ago autism occurred at around one in 10,000 children in the USA, the current figures which are mirrored in the UK are in the region of one in 150 children and this dramatic rise is also been recorded for such conditions as Attention Deficit Hyperactivity Disorder (ADHD), Tourette's syndrome and Obsessive Compulsive Disorder (OCD). For conditions such as dyslexia, dyspraxia and attention deficit it has been suggested the figures could be as high as one child in every five. It has been argued that this dramatic increase is due to altered diagnostic criteria but the fact remains the numbers are rising to epidemic proportions and currently there is no consensus of opinion as to why it is happening.

There may be no consensus of opinion as to the cause of what surely must be considered a terrifying prospect for our children and grandchildren, for the trend would suggest a continuing rise in cases but a growing number of people now believe that it is our lifestyle that is impacting upon the epigenome and triggering the developmental delay. Currently we cannot do anything about maternal or foetal distress – factors implicated in increased probabilities of developmental delay - but we should be aware of how our lives have changed and not necessarily for the better.

Fortunately, it is not necessary to spend several years of training in clinical psychology in order to be a better parental detective and later we will play I Spy (the adult version) and pick up any early signs that may tip the balance and increase the probability that problems just might occur. Here we will relate signs to specific areas of the brain, look at some generalisations and sort the wheat from the chaff as to what is normal in terms of development and what might turn out to be a cause for concern. However, it must be borne in mind that as far as children are concerned nothing is written in stone, there will be wide variations and every child should be an individual in his/her own right. Imagine a world full of sameness!

Dyspraxia

Dyspraxia comes in many shapes and forms, it can be so mild as to pass unnoticed or can impact upon a child's life from a very early necessitating highly skilled professional intervention, be the cause of bullying and even be the underlying cause of flat feet or persistent low back pain. Although, perhaps the earliest manifestation of problems to come is the floppy infant with poor muscle tone, the one thing that grabs the attention of parent and professional alike is speech delay. Oral and verbal dyspraxia is something that will be suspected by the majority of parents of a child with speech delays or problems and is something that few professionals would miss. Certainly in the UK referrals for assessments are the norm if a problem is suspected and the services provided by Speech and Language Therapists are excellent but unfortunately demand may have already exceeded the supply of therapists.

General dyspraxia, which is pretty well universally found in association with the learning and behavioural disorders, is usually seen as clumsiness, a tendency to be accident prone, messy eating habits and poor spatial awareness. Children with a moderate degree of dyspraxia may struggle to achieve the timing, balance and coordination necessary to master the art of riding a bike and may even fail to get to grips with pedalling a tricycle. Such things as catching, throwing or kicking a ball are slow to master or are not mastered at all thereby making sporting activities something the child would prefer to avoid. The lack of gaining such skills can lead to social exclusion by peers, taunting or frank bullying.

Dyspraxia is the sum total of poor gross motor skills (body movements), poor fine motor skills (hand control), poor coordination, poor balance and poor sequencing. How the dyspraxia is manifested will be the result of how the percentages of all of these essential skills are presented. Therefore, the so-called 'dressing dyspraxia' might be purely down to fine motor skills as in an inability to do up buttons or tie laces or poor balance in the child that constantly falls over when lifting one foot off the ground.

The timing of coordinated hand movements is a function of the lower brainstem, contralateral (opposite) cerebellar hemisphere and the upper brainstem. If the two triangular circuits are out of sync either due to the lower brainstems spontaneous pulsations or an under-functioning cerebellar hemisphere, then the two hands will struggle to work together in unison. An under-functioning cerebellar hemisphere may also cause reduced muscle tone on the same side of the body and a greatly reduced ability to balance. Also, as the cerebellum receives a vast amount of feedback concerning what the muscles of the entire body have just done, an under-functioning cerebellar hemisphere may fail to pass on vital information concerning the positioning of the body and the limbs to an area of the brain that has to know exactly where you are at any moment of time before a new movement can be initiated.

The majority of people on the planet will be right-handed and the vast majority of textbooks on the subject will tell you that the control of the right hand is from the left side of the brain. There is now good evidence to suggest that although the left side of the brain does indeed control the right arm, there is a huge contribution from the right hemisphere that make fine motor skills possible and this arises in part from the right mid cingulate gyrus. Therefore, to address issues involving fine motor skills it is necessary to target the medial wall of the right brain.

Dyslexia

The British Dyslexia Association (BDA) provides the following list of indications of dyslexia for parents:-

Indications of Dyslexia

If a child has several of these indications, further investigation should be made. The child may be dyslexic, or there may be other reasons. This is not a checklist.

1. **Persisting factors**

There are many persisting factors in dyslexia, which can appear from an early age. They will still be noticeable when the dyslexic child leaves school.

These include:
- Obvious 'good' and 'bad' days, for no apparent reason.
- Confusion between directional words, e.g. up/down, in/out.
- **Difficulty with sequence,** e.g. coloured bead sequence, later with days of the week or numbers.
- **A family history of dyslexia/reading difficulties.**

2. **Pre-school**

- Has persistent jumbled phrases, e.g. 'cobbler's club' for 'toddler's club'.
- Use of substitute words e.g. 'lampshade' for 'lamppost'.
- Inability to remember the label for known objects, e.g. 'table, chair'.
- Difficulty learning nursery rhymes and rhyming words, e.g. 'cat, mat, sat'.
- Later than expected **speech development.**

Pre-school non-language indicators:

- May have walked early **but did not crawl** - was a 'bottom shuffler' or 'tummy wriggler'.
- Persistent difficulties in **getting dressed efficiently** and putting shoes on the correct feet.
- Enjoys being read to but shows no interest in letters or words.
- Is often accused of **not listening or paying attention.**
- **Excessive tripping, bumping into things and falling over.**
- **Difficulty with catching, kicking or throwing a ball; with hopping and/or skipping.**
- **Difficulty with clapping a simple rhythm.**

3. **Primary school age**

- Has particular difficulty with reading and spelling.
- Puts letters and figures the wrong way round.
- Has difficulty remembering tables, alphabet, formulae etc.

- Leaves letters out of words or puts them in the wrong order.
- Still occasionally confuses 'b' and 'd' and words such as 'no/on'.
- Still needs to use fingers or marks on paper to make simple calculations.
- **Poor concentration.**
- Has problems understanding what he/she has read.
- **Takes longer than average to do written work.**
- Problems processing language at speed.

Primary school age non-language indicators:

- **Has difficulty with tying shoe laces, tie, dressing.**
- Has difficulty telling left from right, order of days of the week, months of the year etc.
- **Surprises you because in other ways he/she is bright and alert.**
- Has a poor sense of direction and still confuses left and right.
- Lacks confidence and has a poor self image.

4. **Aged 12 or over**

As for primary schools, plus:

- Still reads inaccurately.
- Still has difficulties in spelling.
- Needs to have instructions and telephone numbers repeated.
- Gets 'tied up' using long words, e.g. 'preliminary', 'philosophical'.
- Confuses places, times, dates.
- Has difficulty with planning and writing essays.

- Has difficulty processing complex language or long series of instructions at speed.

Aged 12 or over non-language indicators:

- **Has poor confidence and self-esteem.**
- **Has areas of strength as well as weakness.**

I have highlighted certain indicators provided by the BDA to demonstrate the overlap that exists between dyslexia, dyspraxia and attention deficit. The evidence that the learning and behavioural disorders are no more than symptoms, and symptoms that always appear in comorbidity (together) is growing and it is my belief that this is true. Regardless of whether or not your child has been diagnosed with a problem, shows traits or is totally symptom free, there will be indicators that can be picked up that will give clues as to how well the brain is developing. Convergence insufficiency is found to be present in over 30% of children with learning issues but may also, undiagnosed, hold back a child's ability to reach their reading potential. That is, a child that has a reading age in keeping with their chronological age might well have the ability to attain a higher reading age were it not for aspects of convergence insufficiency.

Attention

A child that lacks attention may, as we have already stated, be suffering from an inability to suppress a primitive visual reflex or if the inattention is limited to schoolwork, be telling you they are struggling or conversely the work is insufficiently challenging. At times we all look for diversions when the task in front of us appears daunting – the aforementioned, hereafter referred to as – or the task is so repetitive and boring that it is not worth attending to. Clearly in this situation it is essential to identify exactly what the problem is so that it can be dealt with appropriately, as left unattended it may well end up being labelled attention deficit disorder.

Attention deficit

Parents are often shocked and baffled when they hear from the school that their child is showing all the signs of attention deficit disorder (ADD). Baffled, because at home he can play on his PlayStation for hours without showing any sign of inattention and in fact can be so focused that he is oblivious of anything else, yet in school he is apparently unable to pay attention. This seemingly strange situation is par for the course with many children (and adults) and is due to the under-functioning of an area of the brain that makes it very difficult to remain focused particularly in busy (external) environments. This under-functioning also causes an area just in front of it to cause an obsessive almost addictive pattern of behaviour (internal) where the player of computer games has to reach the next level. This can cause a perfectly 'normal', reasonable adult to sit up all night, constantly having to reach the next level.

Attention deficit hyperactivity disorder

There is no mistaking a truly ADHD child and the clinic often bears witness to the visits of such children but there is often an overlap between attention deficit and hyperactivity as the diagnostic criteria makes clear.

To meet the diagnostic criteria according to the DSM-IV (Diagnostic and statistical Manual of psychiatric disorders) a couple of aspects have to be considered to meet a diagnosis of ADHD:

A) Six (or more) of either -

    1) Inattention

    2) Hyperactivity/Impulsivity Symptoms

- must have persisted for at least six months to a degree that is maladaptive and inconsistent with developmental level:

    1) Inattention

- often fails to give close attention to details or makes careless mistakes in homework, work, or other activities
- often has difficulties sustaining attention in tasks or play activities
- often does not seem to listen when spoken to directly
- often does not follow through instructions and fails to finish schoolwork, chores, or duties in the workplace (not due to oppositional behaviour or failure to understand instructions)
- often has difficulties organising tasks and activities
- often avoids, dislikes or is reluctant to engage in tasks that require sustained mental efforts
- often loses things necessary for tasks or activities (e.g. toys, school assignments, pencils, books)

- is often easily distracted by extraneous stimuli
- is often forgetful in daily activities

2) Hyperactivity/Impulsivity

Hyperactivity

- often fidgets with hands or feet or squirms in seat
- often leaves seat in classroom or in other situations in which remaining seated is expected
- often runs about or climbs excessively in situations in which it is inappropriate (in adolescents or adults, may be limited to subjective feelings of restlessness)
- often has difficulty playing or engaging in leisure activities quietly
- is often "on the go" or often acts as if "driven by a motor"
- often talks excessively

Impulsivity

- often blurts out answers before questions have been completed
- often has difficulty awaiting turn
- often interrupt or intrudes on others (e.g. butts into conversations or games)

B) Some symptoms causing impairment were present before age seven

C) Some impairment from the symptoms is present in two or more settings (e.g. at school and at home)

D) There must be clear evidence of clinically significant impairment in social, academic or occupational functioning

E) Occurrence is not exclusively during the course of a Pervasive Developmental Disorder, Schizophrenia or other Psychotic Disorder

Also, the diet of the hyperactive child needs careful consideration as certain foods/additives can trigger hyper levels of activity that can last for a couple of days. Often within the child's developing make-up there are clues to an addictive nature as the following extract from an email makes clear –

He was always quite a hyper child - more than the others. No concentration skills. It made it very hard as I could not read books to him, as he always had to be moving on to the next activity / toy after a few minutes. He became even more hyper and loud with other children and was always attracted to the ones like himself. TV and computer games kept his attention and still do to this day although he will read and enjoys it. He has always craved sugar and particularly high additive sweets. I suspect these do something to his brain. He always craved coke and Dr Pepper etc and became hyper on it and would find any way to get sweets and things like this. I put him on a natural healthy diet and restricted things but he would go to friends who were allowed everything and binge there. I did try to let him just have free access to sweets thinking reverse psychology but that did not work and he would have just lived on them. Even now he buys and binges on sweets, coke etc and is now smoking cigarettes (rollups) thinking I don't know. Perhaps this is normal teenage stuff.

The last sentence of this extract says it all. There is a great deal of confusion as to what is normal, with parents not recognising warning signs in an otherwise healthy child or conversely attributing all aberrant behaviour as being due to the child's diagnosed condition. There will be glitches in pretty well every child's development and this needs to be identified but also, the child with a diagnosed disorder will demonstrate elements of pure naughtiness.

Oppositional defiance disorder (ODD)

This is when things really do start to go wrong with an ongoing pattern of disobedient, hostile and defiant behaviour towards both parents and figures of authority which goes beyond the bounds of normal childhood behaviour. It is defined as:-

A pattern of negativistic, hostile, and defiant behaviour lasting at least six months, during which four (or more) of the following are present:

- often loses temper
- often argues with adults
- often actively defies or refuses to comply with adults' requests or rules
- often deliberately annoys people
- often blames others for his or her mistakes or misbehaviour
- is often touchy or easily annoyed by others
- is often angry and resentful
- is often spiteful or vindictive

The child with ODD is a nightmare to live with and very difficult to handle with even the best parenting skills and a great deal of love. It is best to deal with the situation (see later) long before this stage of events as unchecked it may develop into a full blown conduct disorder.

Conduct Disorder

A full-blown conduct disorder is marked by a developing pattern of behaviour in which the child/adolescent violates the rights of others and does not comply to the established rules of the society in which they live thereby breaking the law. It is characterised by verbal and actual physical aggression, acts of cruelty and criminal acts. It takes an inordinate amount of love and an extra ordinary person not to give up on a child with a conduct disorder. Again it is essential to pick up the early signs in what might be typical ADHD behaviour and nip it in the bud at that stage, rather than trying to contain the situation once it has escalated.

Tics

Minor facial tics – blinking, grimacing or nose twitching – occur with such frequency in children as to be considered almost a normal developmental stage. It is possible that as part of the anterior cingulate is developing, a particular neuron called the Calcium binding Calretinin cell, might escape (spontaneous activity) causing both facial and vocal tics. Although the precise function of these cells is not known it has been suggested that they may play an important role in the control of the autonomic nervous system and/or be projection neurons to motor centres involved in the production of facial expression and vocalisation.

It is of interest to note that these minor 'normal' tics tend to occur when the child is overtired, excited, stressed or follow pigging-out on junk food. These same factors also exacerbate established tic disorders and of course are closely linked with the sympathetic – flight-or-fight – autonomic nervous system. Again it is important to recognise the early signs and put in place as soon as possible a treatment plan that will address any dietary issues and where possible de-stress the child.

Obsessive Compulsive Disorder (OCD)

When parents are questioned in clinic as to whether their child has any obsessions, rituals or quirky behaviour, they often mention the habit of lining up cars or a well established bedtime routine. If the right side of the brain is a bit slow off the mark in developing as it should, the child will try to avoid things that are new and will put in place structure and routines that will avoid challenging the right side of the brain and because of the familiarity will act as a comforter. At night it is dark, the house can make strange noises and generally the child is alone in their room, hence the need to be made safe by the bedtime ritual.

True OCD is a type of anxiety disorder. Children with OCD become preoccupied with things that could be potentially harmful, dangerous, wrong, or dirty. At times of stress we all perseverate – have a thought that goes round and round in our head that we cannot get rid of – but hopefully this only happens in the short-term. With OCD the thoughts keep on coming and unless something is done, something terrible may happen. Children that start to obsess do not like to talk about it and over a period of time a guilt complex in association with the anxiety and rituals. If a child, often around ten years of age, starts to change becoming less outgoing, a little sullen or snappy, it is time for a cuddle and a quiet chat. The guilt associated with OCD, tic disorders and the low self esteem that many dyslexic children suffer would appear to arise from the same area of the brain towards the front of the cingulate gyrus and is amenable to drug free treatment if caught in time.

Eating disorders

Pica refers to the habit of eating non-food items – soil, paper or uncooked food items – and is most commonly seen in pregnant women and young children. The name for this sometimes worrying habit comes from the Latin word for Magpie, a bird with a reputation for not being a particularly fussy eater. Generally it is not something of great concern unless it persists or the items consumed are likely to be toxic.

Rumination syndrome is said to be a common under-diagnosed complaint that affects infants, children and an increasing numbers of otherwise healthy adolescents and adults. It is characterised by effortless, spontaneous regurgitation of meals. It has been documented in association with cognitive disorders, depression and found to be present in 10% of psychiatric patients in institutions. In children it may therefore indicate a glitch in the maturation of the developing brain.

The way ahead

In this chapter we have looked at the major learning and behavioural disorders and it might be reasonable to ask why in a book about parenting it is necessary to dwell on disorders that will only affect 20% of children. The answer is that every child will have sub-clinical signs of these disorders and they will generate the behaviour which puzzles, challenges or drives parents to distraction. The perfect child of the most perfect parents in theory would not present any cause for concern or need for parental discussions but as that child probably does not exist, we must learn how to pick up the early warning signs and deal with them effectively, plus be able to step back and look at ourselves. Family dynamics, agendas and the strife that these can cause may be the underlying factor that delays development or causes the 'normal' child to run away from home.

8 TOUGH LOVE

Earlier we talked about the reasons for getting married or living together and the type of family that may result from this union. Here, we must look at how that relationship might work and the pressures it may bring to the family and stressors it may place on the youngest members of the family unit. For a child to not only survive, but to thrive, it will require food, drink, warmth, shelter, security, care and love. For the brain to grow normally it needs oxygen, nutrients and an abundance of love. If we think of the child as a seed we want to grow, it is obvious that it will require the right compost, temperature, degree of sunlight and water. Once it is established it will also need feeding, support and perhaps repotting or planting out. It will of course be subject to disease, adverse weather conditions and even vandalism. And so it is with the child.

Our family background may well influence who we eventually end up with and can greatly influence, certainly in terms of expectation, how the family is structured and functions. When and how conception came about can also be important factors in any underlying discord, ongoing stress or extended bliss. The woman who knowingly gets herself pregnant in order to alter the dynamics of a developing relationship could be asking for trouble unless her partner also wanted children early on in the relationship or is incredibly laid-back. The couple who having decided to start a family and find that they can't and eventually follow the IVF route will pass through a long period of not knowing and the stress that this can engender. Conversely, the couple that gets married following months of planning, have the dream honeymoon and soon after discovers that they are to be blessed with a child, may feel quite rightly that they are truly blessed.

Where we live, what we do to earn a living and our finances can have a dramatic impact upon family life and the opportunities and freedom that can be offered to the child. Living on a crime ridden estate with drug dealers on every corner and gangs wandering the streets is not the best environment to bring up children and limits their freedom of movement. Conversely, those fortunate enough to live in a more rural setting may have literally acres of space to play in and the opportunity to have pets or even a pony. The type of property we live in may also be a factor providing for both good and bad. A detached property in a quiet cul-de-sac may mean that there are other children to play with in a relatively safe environment, whereas a semi-detached house with the neighbour from hell can generate stress because you feel you have to keep the children quiet or suffer noise pollution yourself.

Background and income can make a huge difference to the life experiences the child can expect to enjoy or endure. If you were packed off to boarding school at an early age, it may well be that you will decide to put your child's name down shortly after birth. Going through the route to public schooling or receiving a private education will no doubt open doors later in life and will certainly provide you with a first class education in schools that provide small class sizes and endless facilities. Living on an estate in a poorer area of the country will provide you with few options as to which school your child attends and there are certainly going to be more than 12 pupils in the class. Class size, facilities on offer and special needs provision are often factors given considerable consideration by parents that can afford to buy an education.

Income, will not only influence where you live and the property you live in but will also impact upon the social circles in which you mix and activities that you indulge in and this will of course open up a world of opportunities to your children. Having land or living in a rural setting may provide the opportunity of owning a pony, joining the pony club and for the child to be exposed to a particular lifestyle. Income and location may also make dinghy sailing an option and a large family powerboat can bring distance horizons within reach. Owning a pony or a dog and being able to walk safely through the countryside may provide children with a life enriching experience that a child living in an inner city can only dream of.

The size of the bank balance will also be a deciding factor in the type and frequency of family holidays. A holiday may be just a few days out with mum and dad visiting local attractions, a week in Benidorm or skiing just after Christmas, getting away at Easter and several weeks during the summer spent at the family house in the South of France. Again, the life experiences a child is exposed to just by going on holiday to Blackpool for a week as opposed to a fortnight in the Maldives or weeks in a rural setting in France will be very different and will affect the developing child.

How the family income is derived will also, often insidiously, affect the child and shape their destiny. The family from a wealthy background will have a particular lifestyle and will have either very fixed expectations, as in working in the family business and/or the city or conversely who needs good A-level passes, providing you can speak nicely. The knowledge that a small fortune, held in trust, will be available on reaching 18 years of age means that there is no pressure to get a good job and often no family expectation.

The low-income family may not be able to provide much more than the basic essentials, may have to settle for a school with a poor reputation, will not have the finance or facilities to even consider having a pony and may struggle to pay the bills. A low income can produce a variety of stressors in a child's life from the quality of food available to family arguments as to what little money they have should be spent on or the inevitable row when the gas bill or mobile phone bill hits the doormat. Having to scrimp and save, having to cut corners and buy cheaper and perhaps less wholesome food is not something the medium to high earner has to consider and yet these simple everyday facts of life will impact upon the development of countless children.

Background and income will dictate what, when and where a child will eat and it is often the life experiences of the parents that will be projected upon the child or children of the family. Where you shop, be it Tesco or Harrods, what you buy, how you cook and where you dine will be a product of your upbringing and even the Nouveau riche will struggle to conceal their more humble beginnings. While some children would not be phased by pheasant or escargot, others would bulk at the very idea. Again, location will play a great part in what is accepted as being normal and while we make associate the eating of pheasant with the lord of the manor, this would be in error as many country folk of lesser standing eat this meat on a regular basis.

Particularly in the case of lower income families the type of food purchased and the likely quality of the food in terms of both nutritional value and contents will be influenced not only by shopping habits but also special offers and just how much money there is to go around. The advent of the supermarket, shelf-life and availability of foods that would in the past be out of season has dramatically altered what we consume. Unfortunately, many foods now contain high levels of sugar, salt and fat and who knows if strawberry flavour or strawberry flavoured yoghurt actually contains strawberries. Supermarkets and their array of processed, oven-ready or microwavable meals and the ever increasing fast food outlets have changed the way a great many people eat and what we feed our children. Most towns and cities will have a street or streets that are lined with kebab shops and other food outlets often designed to attract late night revellers. If you have ever doubted that the meals these outlets provide might not be too good for you, walk the streets in daylight and note well the pavements stained with fat.

Changing structure

For many families the structure and function of the unit is not fixed and is subject to both expected and unexpected changes. Being in the Armed Forces with long tours of duty, working on an oil-rig or being a long-distance lorry driver, can mean that for variable periods of time the family is reduced to being a 'single-parent' family. Regardless of a child's development, there will always be times when the presence of an alpha male is required, not just as a role model but also to enforce discipline. For other families it may not just be a matter of daddy being away lots on business, as work and/or promotion may mean relocating to a different part of the country or actually moving abroad. This can be very unsettling for a child, as moving home is a known major stressor but may also involve having to learn a second language.

The working mum

The single mother may need to work, the mother in a low income family may have to work to supplement the income and the mother with a profession may choose to return to work. In each case, the absence of the mother for periods of the day, evening or even the night will involve either fitting the hours of work in between dropping the kids off to school and picking them up and that can be fraught with problems particularly during times of illness, school holidays, inset days or by the demands of an unsympathetic boss. In each case, having to work or returning to work, will inevitably involve a third party and this to some extent will involve loss of control as to what the child is fed, activities undertaken or what they are exposed to.

The second child

The arrival of the second child should be a time of great joy but can be marred if the first-born child feels that their nose has been put out of joint. Occasionally, this can lead to real problems and it has been known for the first-born to harm the new arrival. Generally this situation can be avoided if the first-born is involved right from the start so that they feel not only important but also that they have a vital role to play in the bringing up of their little brother or sister. It is essential that the first-born is given 'special time' so that they do not feel pushed out by the new arrival and that time is set aside each day just for them and that days out are arranged when dad can take them off to somewhere special.

Pecking order

In days gone by it was usual for the man of the house, the bread winner, to be master in his own house. Times have changed but in many households this remains true to this day. In various religious groups, from Muslim to Mormon, it is the man of the house that must be obeyed, while in certain parts of the country the old traditions remain firmly in place. However, in many families today, decision making is equally shared between the partners regardless of who is actually going out to work, as the role of homemaker and mother is regarded as equally important. Indeed, in some families the role is swopped and if the mother wishes to return to work or it makes more economic sense for her to work, then it is the male that runs the home and undertakes bringing up the children.

Regardless of the family set-up it is essential to realise that each partner also has a more animalistic role to play in ensuring that the family functions as it should. Earlier we talked about neurotransmitters and the impact they may have upon behaviour. We must also bear in mind that children are also subject to varying levels of neurotransmitters and hormones and this can present as a major problem within the day to day family dynamics unless it is appreciated and dealt with appropriately. Boys have three puberties, one shortly after birth, one at about 10-11 years and the major one when they potentially turn into Kevin's in the early teens. During the second puberty, many boys empowered by the surge of testosterone, decide to challenge the authority of their mother and either answerback or refuse to obey her requests. It is at this stage, regardless of the family set-up, that the alpha male needs to assert his hormonal authority.

That a pecking order exists might seem abhorrent to some modern minded people but at least as far as neurotransmitters and hormones are concerned it is a reality. When something goes bump in the night or an emergency occurs by day, it is most likely that the alpha male will be expected to deal with it. The male of the species is generally bigger, stronger and potentially more aggressive and is therefore more likely to survive and triumph in a situation of danger. However, it is not just in situations of danger that the alpha male needs to exert his authority and a visit to the zoo will soon demonstrate how throughout the animal kingdom the male must at times ensure that the children at least know who is boss.

Setting boundaries

Pretty well every society will have established rules and regulations most of which will be established in law. Within society, there will be accepted sub groups based on ethnic origin and/or religious beliefs, groups that may be tolerated even though their behaviour may border on unlawful and still others that live permanently on the wrong side of the law. Muslims are lawful people that have a faith built on peace and strong family values. Romanies also have strong family ties, strict codes of conduct, if perhaps a slight disregard of the law at times. Hardened criminals may have what appears to be a total disregard for the laws of the land but most observe a strict code of ethics with regard to crimes against women, children and the elderly. It is for this reason that certain prisoners are segregated for their own safety.

Each family has to set boundaries and limitations to behaviour based on ethnic background, religious faith and family history. That is, immigrant families may bring with them a more tolerant attitude to children, while deeply religious families may limit the activities their children may engage in, while unfortunately some parents appear to have no concern whatsoever as to where and what their children are up to. All children need to be aware of danger, have set boundaries and to know right from wrong. This has to be established at an early age as once the child is as big as and stronger than his mother it may well be too late.

Danger to children takes many forms and ranges from potential dangers in the home to stranger danger and the perils of an out of control child near a busy street. In the home a child must learn that things can burn, that electricity is dangerous and that certain items are poisonous. In this day and age, children need to be taught at an early age that they must not talk to strangers either directly or via the internet and certainly must not go with them if asked. Some children take a delight in ignoring their parent's orders oblivious to the danger they are placing themselves in. If a child is running away from their parents, they must stop when asked, well before reaching a busy street or they face the potential of becoming a statistic.

Law and order

Very young children can be taught the meaning of 'hot' or 'it will burn' and this needs to be achieved to prevent accidents in the home. Similarly, outside the home children must be aware of the danger of traffic and how to cross a road safely, but also children need to be taught and learn by example how they must behave both within the family and within society. Once a child is able to crawl, the basic rules need to be put in place and as they move through the various stages of development the appropriate etiquette, form and behaviour should be established. Table manners, awaiting your turn and appropriate responses need to be put in place as a child learns new skills not once they have already established very bad habits. If you find swearing, belching or passing wind in public acceptable, the chances are that your children will do the same and therefore standards need to be set across the board.

Reward v punishment

If appropriate standards of behaviour are taught right from the start there should be little reason to question as to whether reward or punishment is the best way to get a child to behave. However, as working towards a goal is something we all have to do at times it is well to set in place deferred gratification at the earliest possible age. Young children have a limited ability to understand concepts of time, therefore telling a child they cannot have something today but they can have it next week is the same as speaking in double-dutch. Once you have said 'No' the rest of the sentence is superfluous as the words used to describe time are meaningless and the chances are you are about to witness a tantrum borne of frustration. Therefore, it is essential to put the basics of law and order in place at an early age so that the child knows that 'No' means 'No' and that a dialogue does not follow. Once you allow the child to start a dialogue or argument you have lost control.

If a child breaches the established code of conduct within the family, they must be told immediately that what they have said or done is not acceptable and be told not to do it again. For most children being confronted by an adult is sufficient to alert them to the error of their ways and should prevent further misdemeanours, however, should the child not respond to a verbal warning or if the behaviour persists, they must be punished immediately. Although there may be a great temptation to give a naughty child a slap on their backside, it is not the answer and if witnessed it could be you that is in trouble with the law.

When telling a child off it is necessary to go down to their physical level, gain eye contact and move into their personal space before quietly and calmly telling them what they have done wrong and what the consequences are to be. Again, it is imperative that you do not allow the child to engage you in a dialogue. If the telling off involves a warning regarding future behaviour it is essential that you stick to your guns and carry through what you have said. Children are by nature fast learners and they will very quickly pick up on idle threats. Saying ten times over "If you do that again I am going to ………. " is just a waste of your breath, therefore say what you mean and mean what you say.

The Naughty Step

Made famous by Super Nanny the 'Naughty Step' is an effective means of cooling down a situation and correcting inappropriate behaviour. Sending a child to their room in most cases just means they can get on with some other activity or if really wound up, trash the place. The naughty step if applied correctly makes the child remain still for a set period of time – a minute for each year of their age – gives them time to cool off and requires them to say sorry for what they have done. If the child is overexcited, hyperactive or just disobedient it may be necessary to put the child back on the step on several occasions before they comply. Once the child is on the step nobody should talk to them or pass by them, as it is important that they remain alone in silence for the set period of time. At the end of the punishment the child must say sorry for what they have done before giving mum or dad a hug so that both parties realise the punishment is over and the misdemeanour forgiven.

The child's room – their personal space/world

Whenever possible a child should have their own bedroom set up as they desire so that they have somewhere to go to be quiet but also somewhere where they feel safe and secure. As mentioned earlier, as the brain develops it is likely that the right side will struggle more than the left and as it is the right side that has to confront anything new, if it is a bit off-colour then it needs the familiarity and security that the personal space, one's own little world can provide. Children that are not feeling too well or who are upset will often retreat to their room to handle familiar objects or simply curl up in their own bed. A child's use of their personal space can provide much useful information to a parent and can provide early warning signs of minor OCD traits, how they are coping with tics or if something has gone wrong at school. N.B. It also provides the opportunity for some child to spend too much time on their computer, avoid homework or source undesirable websites.

9 A TANGLED WEB

The dysfunctional family

A family may simply not work for a variety of reasons and here we must attempt to identify some of the more common causes of dysfunction and the stressors that the breakdown may engender. Life, Fate, whatever you want to call it can place you in a situation that is not of your making and from which it appears there is no escape. However, in many situations there are changes that can be made or strategies that can be put in place that will at least ameliorate the situation if not correct it.

The single parent

The single parent scenario can be by choice, divorce or death of a partner but in each case it will present its own set of challenges. With sex education freely and widely available it may appear to some that clearly getting pregnant is a matter of choice but it would appear that to many young people there is a mind-set that either says this is not going to happen to me or I really don't care. Indeed, some young people see pregnancy as a natural stage towards gaining housing and starting adult life usually at the expense of the state. Perhaps it should not come as too much of a surprise when the father of the child decides that he is not ready to settle down leaving the very expectant mother to fend for herself.

A single mother may have financial constraints, will have limited personal freedom and will lack a father figure for her child. There may also be guilt associated with wanting time away from the child and conflicts should another male partner discipline her child. Relative poverty, being housebound and lacking the emotional security of a long-term partner does not make for the best start to bringing up a child. Also, the mind-set that the world owes me a living and that I should have every conceivable electronic gadget in my home, does not create the foundations for a work ethic and intrinsic honesty, that is, to be reliant upon one's own abilities, to strive to be the best that we can be and to be honest with ourself.

Liberal

The family unit should be a model of the society in which we live preparing us for our survival once we are ready to leave home and live independently. Apart from the very basic life skills of learning to wash and dress ourselves etc., we must also learn what is acceptable within that society in terms of common decency, manners and advanced social skills. The advanced social skills should prepare us to deal with a wide variety of social situations from a casual chat with both friends and strangers to a formal job interview. In each situation, we have to know exactly how to behave, what is expected of us, the interpersonal boundaries that exist and we must be able to rapidly read a changing social situation so that we can respond appropriately.

Each person that we have contact with will have their own personal space and their own mental distance. That is, we can come into close personal contact with parents, friends and lovers – enter their personal space – and talk to them about a variety of subjects that an acquaintance or stranger might feel uncomfortable with – mental distance. To a great part we learn these physical and mental skills unconsciously, only occasionally needing to be corrected by a parent when we have gone too far. To achieve the advanced levels of social skills we need a good teacher, exposure to a variety of social situations and a fully functioning prefrontal cortex. Without set boundaries even the perfectly functioning cortex will struggle to get things right and unacceptable behaviour will ensue.

Children need boundaries not only to fit in with the dictates of the society in which we live but also to excel in every social situation. Being popular and having friends is important to children and those lacking in even the basic social skills will struggle to act appropriately and as a consequence may be shunned by their peers. Many children that struggle to fit in will attempt to befriend someone that they feel is also struggling, mix with the naughtier children or become the class clown thereby turning their inability to cope to their advantage.

Should a child have a borderline learning or behavioural issue, let alone a diagnosed developmental delay, it is essential to establish at an early age just where the boundaries lie and just what is acceptable behaviour. A failure to do so may lead to oppositional behaviour when the child is not only older but bigger, making it impossible to control them either verbally or physically. Should the oppositional behaviour escalate into a conduct disorder, when the police are likely to be involved, it may prove impossible for the family unit to cope or the child to be helped.

Great expectations

The family that is lax in setting standards of behaviour and establishing fixed boundaries may well be making a rod for their own back but the family that is too rigid in their application of standards may well make their own life easier but at the expense of their children. In many ways, we need to learn by our mistakes and that requires a certain degree of freedom and the opportunity to profit from our errors. One of the many functions of the anterior cingulate is error correction and like the rest of the brain it needs to practice this function in order to have ability to see the errors of our way. Clearly, this must not mean putting the child at risk but must occur for the child to develop the independent ability to make value judgements.

At times we all feel like wrapping our children in cotton wool to protect them from the evils of the world but whenever possible we must allow them the freedom to learn the necessary life skills so that they can grow in confidence and develop a positive self image. Whether it is making a new friend, making the right choice or learning a new skill, children need to have the reigns loosened off and the apron strings untied in order to have the opportunity to learn the hard way. We need to set good examples and be good role models but we cannot do everything for our children, some things children have to experience for themselves.

Some parents are determined that their child/children are going to have everything that they feel they missed out on in their childhood but often forget that as wonderful as material possessions can be that they cannot replace time spent with the children and the obvious joy this engenders. Often it is necessary to work long hours to earn the cash to fund an extravagant lifestyle and the absences and the overtired parent that ignores the children may not realise that they are being counterproductive. Sometimes it is better to spend a couple of hours together doing something perhaps a little challenging so that afterwards the father and son can bathe in the afterglow of the achievement. There is no replacement for quality time.

It is not only lifestyle that may be thrust upon the child but also the type of education. Some children, regardless of their state of development, will be packed off to boarding school at a very early age simply because that is what one does. To some it may appear totally illogical to go through the whole process of pregnancy, labour and delivery, only to dump the child at the earliest opportunity into the care of others. It might be argued that no child is ready for such a traumatic separation from the family and certainly some children will suffer as a consequence. Such a decision should be viewed from the child's perspective and how being suddenly separated from particularly the mother may leave permanent scars.

Other parents want their children to have the educational opportunities that they feel they missed out on and if finances permit will buy an education for their child. Generally speaking such a decision is to be admired but it should be borne in mind that many of the children attending the school will come from exceptionally wealthy families with lifestyles and properties that most people can only dream of while thumbing through a glossy magazine. Although in theory the child should receive a first rate education, being the child that lives in the smallest house, who doesn't have a pony and doesn't have three holidays a year, can be a source of much unhappiness. Also, if the chosen school has a reputation for high academic success it may be that the child cannot cope and ends up struggling in the bottom set.

All children should be safe, happy and given the opportunity to reach their particular potential but sometimes the expectations of the parents may exceed the child's capability. Not all children can be educational high-fliers and just because everyone in the past has entered medicine or become a lawyer, it does not mean that the latest addition to the family has the ability to enter chambers. Selecting the right school for your child, providing a private tutor or subscribing to any of the excellent teaching programmes available online may well help a child to reach their potential in life but they can only do their best and to expect more is not realistic and may put the child under undue pressure.

CASE HISTORY 8 - Mary aged 8, not achieving

Mary was born at full-term by an unassisted natural delivery. She passed through all the developmental stages perfectly on time and was a happy sociable child. However, once into Reception she struggled to learn to read, could not spell and reversed certain numbers, letters and words. When seen in clinic her reading ability was that of a five year old.

Following the consultation and examination it became clear that Mary was somewhat dyspraxic, struggled to remain focused and was suffering from secondary dyslexia as she could not bring her eyes into convergence let alone track smoothly. This was music to her father's ears as he was convinced there must be a reason why his daughter was struggling with the very basics of learning.

Her father was a well educated, highly successful business man that clearly doted on his only child. Clearly, he wanted the best for Mary and once the convergence, tracking and visual focus had been dealt with, brought in a host of tutors and set up a timetable that included two hours of tuition each weekday evening together with his own input at weekends. Each day he would collect her from school and ferry her to the various tutors, never leaving her side until she had read the bedtime story and settled down to sleep.

Although Mary's reading age soon caught up with her chronological age and she stopped reversing numbers and letters, her father was clearly agitated that she was not excelling at school. All the extra tuition that had been put in place left little time just to be a little girl and the strain of constantly being under pressure was beginning to show. When Mary had first attended the clinic, she could not read but at least she laughed when teased and had a smile that lit up the room. Now she sat with her head bowed and remained unresponsive to anything other than direct questioning. While her father was contemplating moving Mary to a different school and bringing in still more tutors, it was suggested that perhaps it would be a good idea to take Mary to see an Educational Psychologist for an assessment. Although Mr X said he thought that would be a good idea, his body language was saying that his daughter didn't need such an assessment.

That was the last time that Mary was seen in clinic. It is of interest to note that although Mr X had spoken to his wife on a couple of occasions while in clinic, she did not attend the clinic from start to finish and I wondered just how much of her daughter she was allowed to have.

Divorce

This final act that causes the destruction of the family unit can follow months or years of continual arguments, can be the rational decision of a couple that have simply grown apart or can be a sudden violent response to a partner caught with their pants down. In each case it is the children that will ultimately suffer either as a result of exposure to months of sometimes violent arguments or the sudden departure of a parent and all that follows. Some parents will stay together for the sake of the children but if the interactions between the parents are tempestuous we have to ask the question, is this the right environment in which to bring up children? Similarly, if the marriage is loveless, lacking any signs of affections and physical contact between the parents, are we presenting the right role models for the children? Children need to live in a harmonious family unit and to witness a working relationship where their parents hold hands, kiss and cuddle and laugh together.

No matter how it comes about the chances are that divorce will affect the children and in many ways it is probably better, if it is inevitable, to get it over as quickly as possible. Unfortunately, the trauma of divorce does not end with the decree absolute and is often the starting point of a whole new ball game of stressors. There may need to be a move to a smaller more affordable house, financial problems and endless irate phone calls and further visits to court to settle access. In this process the children will suffer the stress of moving, perhaps loss of friends and perhaps having to settle for a much smaller bedroom or even having to share a room. During this transition period, finances may be limited, maintenance not paid or financial burdens may be put in place by an embittered ex that causes the mother (usually) to become angry and upset. There is no way that the children in this situation can avoid the stress of seeing their mother crying or taking the flack that follows an upsetting phone call.

Once arrangements for reasonable access are in place there is always a potential for stress pockets when the children have to physically move from their home with mum to dad's house and perhaps meeting his new partner. Depending upon how the marriage ended the points in time when the parents have to meet can be trigger points for digs at one another or the opportunity for the father to taunt their ex with his new car or new woman. The weekend with dad can also be an opportunity to get one over on the mother who is struggling financially, by buying the children expensive gifts or purposely ignoring requests not to buy the children sweets and junk food. It is a sad fact of life that many embittered divorcees will use the children as weapons in an attempt to hurt their ex partner.

CASE HISTORY 9 - Tug of love? Mark aged 8

Mark's mother made an appointment for me to see him and then promptly cancelled it. Within a week she had rebooked and was on the verge of cancelling again when she changed her mind once more and went ahead with it. I expect parents to be a little apprehensive and nervous initially, but this lady was a nervous breakdown on legs. Her words came out as though fired from a machine gun, a right-sided facial tic punctuating the stressful story she was relating, and her hands constantly performed the most elaborated ritual of wringing movements. Every time her ex-husband's name was mentioned her head would make a sudden turn to the side to accompany an exaggerated facial tic.

*We had been talking – she had been talking – for nearly twenty minutes and as yet there had been no mention of Mark, his problems or her concerns for him. At this point I took control of the situation and gently but firmly directed the conversation, now at last a dialogue, towards the purpose of the visit. In a nutshell, Mark was beginning **to struggle at school**, had become **very emotional** and had started **wetting the bed** on a nightly basis.*

*The family history was dominated by her ex-husband's obsessive behaviour, not only as a child but within the confines of the marriage, which she felt had contributed greatly to the marital breakdown. Mark had been born at full-term by natural delivery and, apart from the fact that the cord was around his neck, the birth had gone like clockwork. He had attained all his developmental milestones pretty well on time apart from gaining **bladder control**. He was over three before being more or less dry by day and over five before becoming dry at night.*

*He had always been a **nervous child**, needing constant reassurance, and would frequently wake at night having had a bad dream. Calling out for his mother, he would enter his parent's bedroom and attempt to get into bed with his mother. His boarding-school-educated father considered this to be totally unnecessary behaviour and would shout at Mark, ordering him back to bed.*

Mark had coped at school, clearly trying to the best of his ability, until the separation and divorce of his parents. From then on the bed-wetting returned and his schoolwork suffered badly. Not surprisingly under the circumstances, his mother found it increasingly difficult to cope with Mark and the situation was compounded by his father's almost Victorian attitude to his son's problems. This very soon produced a situation where Mark refused to visit his father when it was his weekend to have him, thus fuelling further acrimonious accusations from him against his ex-wife.

The first thing Mark needed was a mate, and a very powerful alpha male at that. Well, we didn't have one of those, so he would have to make do with me. We arranged that he would call me a couple of times a week, supposedly to discuss how the treatment was going. In fact, we talked about everything except his treatment, with me slipping 'That's really cool' into the dialogue as often as I could. The treatment itself involved strict dietary changes, including no bad E-numbers and artificial sweeteners, plus the addition of omega-3 and omega-6 and some physical and computer generated programs.

At first all went well. Within ten days the bed-wetting had stopped and his mother confirmed, what I had gathered from our chats on the phone, that his level of confidence was growing on a daily basis. In fact things were going so well that when his father insisted on having Mark for the weekend, he had agreed and gone off quite happily.

When he returned on the Sunday evening he was quiet, on edge and went straight to his room. His mother could get nothing from him other than, 'It's nothing, leave me alone.' That next day his father was on the phone to inform her that he had flushed the omega-3 and omega-6 down the toilet, wanted to know why she was starving him and wanted my telephone number as somebody needed to stop this quack messing up young kids.

Apparently, apart from flushing the omega capsules down the loo, he had insisted on Mark eating good old-fashioned junk food, washed down with a well-known brand of fizzy drink, had ridiculed the exercise programme and had taken away Mark's laptop, thus preventing him from doing his eye exercises. Needless to say, I had a very distraught mother on the phone in floods of tears asking what she could do.

Fortunately, the problem was taken out of our hands when Mark decided that he would not visit his father again if he had to eat junk food and could not do his exercises. Faced with this ultimatum, eventually his father conceded and over a period of time not only helped Mark to stick to his regime, but started taking omega capsules himself. I am still awaiting the phone call.

(Taken from chapter 12 of Is That My Child? *Virgin Books)*

Adoption

Most of us when we were younger had to give careful thought to contraception and as many a young girl has discovered to her cost it is all too easy to get pregnant. Not so for some couples who discover over a period of time, that having tried for a baby, they are unable to make their lives complete and have that much wanted child. Some couples have to go down the route of IVF before their dream comes true but for others their options become very limited. For some it is possible to conceive via sperm or egg donation, while others finally have to consider adoption and all that it entails. The problem with these last two decisions is that you cannot be certain as to what you are taking on either from a genetic perspective and/or as to what the child may have been exposed to.

Adoption is never going to be easy, will involve endless red-tape and interviews, may be expensive and even if you are a millionaire superstar may not be straightforward. If you are fortunate enough to be able to offer a child a home that is full of love, you cannot be certain of that child's future as they will probably come with a very limited history. Some children that are offered up for adoption will be in that position because their mother was a drug addict, was an alcoholic or neglected their baby. In this situation, the child may have been scarred for life and even if they have managed to survive the abuse unscathed, may well have been affected simply by the process of fostering and adoption.

In the following chapters we will attempt to provide a means to identify potential problems in the child's development as early as possible together with the early warning signs that the family is not functioning at its optimal level, before suggesting strategies that can be put in place to ease the burden on the children once the family unit has broken up.

10 I SPY

In this chapter we will look at how we may be able to predict the likelihood of problems developing in the child, consider the probability that one or both parents may themselves have a developmental issue and look for signs that the family dynamics may be under undue stress. To do this we will look at various known stressors and by identifying patterns of signs or symptoms consider the probability that steps need to be taken to ameliorate the situation.

In each of the following sections we will create a score for the child/children, parents and family that should help to identify where problems may lie and thereby open up the possibility of addressing specific issues that are causing unnecessary stress within the daily life of the family unit and potentially hindering its growth and development.

If the answer to any of the following questions is 'YES', note down the question number and the number of 'YES's applicable (e.g. A1 = 2)

Ticking the boxes

Identifying problems in the child

(Complete this section for each child)

A1
- Is there a history of developmental delay in either side of the family?
- Is there a history of developmental delay on the father's side?
- Was the mother unwell during the pregnancy?
- Is there a history of mental illness on either side of the family?
- Would you describe the birth of any of your children as difficult?

(Developmental Delay is dyslexia, dyspraxia, ADD, ADHD, OCD or a tic disorder in patterns of comorbidity)

A2
- Did your child suffer foetal distress?
- Did you have a Ventouse delivery (suction)?
- Did you have a forceps assisted birth?
- Was the cord around the neck?
- Was meconium present?

A3
- Did your child sit unaided later than 6 months?
- Did your baby not crawl?
- Was your child late walking (> 1 yr)?
- Did your child have a speech delay?
- Was your child late becoming dry day and/or night?

A4

- Did your child lack imaginative play?
- Did your child struggle to socialise at playschool?
- Was your child ever aggressive towards other children?
- Did your child soil themselves?
- Did your child suffer separation anxiety?

A5

- Once in Reception did your child struggle to read?
- Does your child struggle with spellings?
- Does you child struggle with maths?
- Does your child have poor handwriting?
- When writing does their hand/arm ache?

A6

- Was your child late riding a bike?
- Is your child accident prone?
- Has your child ever been clumsy?
- Does your child have poor spatial awareness?
- Did your child struggle to learn to dress themselves?

A7

- Does your child have a poor short-term memory?
- Does your child struggle to concentrate?
- Is your child impulsive?
- Does your child struggle to keep still?
- Is your child active / hyperactive?

A8

- Does your child have any rituals?
- Is your child obsessed with anything?
- Does your child prefer routine?
- Does your child watch certain videos repeatedly?

- Does your child ask the same question repeatedly?

A9
- Has you child ever had a facial tic (blinking/grimacing)?
- Has your child ever had a vocal tic (throat clearing, squeaking, etc.)?
- Has your child ever had a motor tic (movement of head, limb or body)?
- Has your child ever made inappropriate comments or sworn?
- Does your child repeat what you have said?

A10
- Did your child ever walk on tiptoe?
- Has your child ever flapped their hands?
- Does your child struggle to maintain eye contact?
- Does your child shun affection?
- Is your child obsessed with spinning objects?

A11
- Is your child struggling in school?
- Are there behavioural issues at school?
- Does your child have a low level of self esteem (I'm rubbish)?
- Is your child failing to reach their potential?
- Have you been contacted by the school?

A12
- Has your child had asthma?
- Has your child had eczema?
- Has your child had any recurrent infections?
- Has your child had numerous accidents?
- Has your child had any serious illnesses?

A13
- Does your child prefer cereals / toast for breakfast?
- Does your child eat sweets on a daily basis?
- Does your child have a restricted diet?
- Does your child eat a lot of junk food?
- Does your child drink fizzy drinks?

A14
- Does your child have tantrums?
- Is your child disobedient?
- Is your child verbally or physically aggressive towards you?
- Does your child refuse to do what he/she is told?
- Is your child easily upset?

A15
- Does your child have a poor relationship with his/her mother?
- Does your child have a poor relationship with his/her father?
- Does your child struggle to get on with their siblings?
- Does your child struggle to make friends?
- Has your child ever been bullied?

Identifying problems in the adult

(Complete this section for each parent)

B1
- Is there a history of developmental delay in the family?
- Have you been diagnosed with a learning/behavioural problem?
- Were you a late developer?
- Did you struggle at school?
- Did you struggle to make friends?

B2
- Were you a bed wetter?
- Do you still struggle with spelling?
- Do you not enjoy reading?
- Is maths a problem?
- Do you have poor handwriting?

B3
- Were you late learning to ride a bike?
- Are you accident prone?
- Are you clumsy?
- Do you have poor spatial awareness?
- Are you a messy eater?

B4
- Do you have a poor short-term memory?
- Do you find it difficult to concentrate?
- Are you a bit of a fidget?
- Do you struggle to remain still for long periods?
- Do you struggle to maintain eye contact?

B5
- Have you ever had a tic?
- When nervous does your face twitch?
- Does your partner have a tic?
- When nervous does you partner have any habits?
- Do you struggle to speak in public?

B6
- Do you have any rituals?
- Do you have to double-check before leaving the house?
- Do you have any obsessions?
- Are you superstitious?
- Do you have repetitive thoughts?

B7
- Do you drink too much?
- Do you gamble?
- Have you used recreational drugs?
- Do you spend hours playing computer games?
- Do you like fizzy drinks?

B8
- Have you suffered a long-term illness?
- Have you had a mental illness?
- Do you suffer from travel sickness?
- Are you unhappy at times?
- Is your life incomplete?

Identifying problems in the family

C1
- Is the house too small?
- Do you struggle to pay the bills?
- Do you have problems with your neighbours?
- Is it unsafe for the children to play outside?
- Would you move house if you could?

C2
- Have you been divorced?
- Have you been divorced more than once?
- Does your partner flirt?
- Do you have any nagging doubts about your partner?
- Has your partner ever been unfaithful?

C3
- Have you ever searched through your partner's handbag/wallet?
- Have you ever checked your partner's computer?
- Do you check Facebook/Twitter?
- Have you searched through your partner's clothes?
- Have you looked at your partner's mobile phone?

C4
- Does your partner have any annoying habits
- Has your partner stopped making an effort over personal appearance?
- Has your partner put on weight?
- Is personal hygiene an issue?
- Is your partner lazy?

C5
- Has the spark gone out of your relationship?
- Do you avoid having sex?

- Has sex become unimportant to you?
- Is there a sexual act that you avoid?
- Are there any sexual conflicts?

C6

- Do you have a poor work record?
- Have you lost your job more than three times?
- Do you have problems at work?
- Is your job stressful?
- Do you hate Mondays?

C7

- Does your job take you away from home?
- Are you happier when away from home?
- Given the opportunity would you have an affair while away?
- Do you take a greater pride in your appearance while away?
- Are you a different person while away?

C8

- Do you have frequent rows?
- Are there ever periods of silence?
- Do you swear in front of the children?
- Are you verbally aggressive?
- Have you ever been physically aggressive?

C9

- Is your partner rude about you in company?
- Is your partner an embarrassment?
- Has the spark left your relationship?
- Have you fallen out of love?
- Do you fantasise about someone else?

C10
- Do you argue over the children?
- Do you have differences concerning discipline?
- Does your partner seem indifferent to the children?
- Is it always you that attends parent's evenings?
- Does your partner over indulge the children?

C11
- Have there been any problems while on holiday?
- Does your partner do their own thing while on holiday?
- Are things easier in terms of getting on while on holiday?
- Does your partner drink too much while on holiday?
- Does your partner get frustrated with the children?

C12
- Do you wish you could have more days out together?
- Is it too expensive to have days out?
- Do you wish your partner would take the kids out more?
- Does your partner fail to involve the kids?
- Would your partner rather go to the pub than play football?

C13
- Do you bottle things up?
- Do you conceal financial worries?
- Do you not speak about intimate matters?
- Do you have any secrets?
- Do you hide any post from your partner?

C14
- Do you enter into arguments with your children?
- Are there constant battles with the children?

- Do you not have a bedtime for the children?
- Do you not have disciplinary measures in place e.g. naughty step?
- Do you lack control over the older children?

C15
- Do any of the children smoke?
- Do any of the children drink alcohol?
- Do any of the children have unsavoury friends?
- Do any of the children stay out too late?
- Have your children ever stolen money from you?

C16
- Do the younger children mimic an older child's behaviour?
- Do the children hurt each other?
- Are any of the children cruel to animals?
- Do any of the children have recurrent illnesses?
- Do the younger children swear?

C17
- Is it stressful when relatives visit?
- Are you envious of your relatives?
- Do you have a relative living with you?
- Does the resident relative cause problems?
- Are you unable to visit close relatives?

What does it all mean?

<u>The A's</u>

Two or more 'YES's in A1 raises the probability that one or more of your children could have a developmental delay. One 'YES' in A2 increases the probability of developmental delay. One or more 'YES's in A3/4 again add to the probability. One or more 'YES's in A5 would indicate a learning disability, while one or more 'YES's in A6 would add the probability of there being dyspraxia as well. As dyspraxia is the most common comorbid sign to all the learning/behavioural conditions it should come as no surprise if this is present.

One or more 'YES's in A7 indicate that your child is struggling to maintain mental concentration and/or that a primitive defensive visual reflex has been retained. Two or more 'YES's in A8 may indicate that the right side of the brain is struggling to develop or that OCD traits may be present. If there are also two or more 'YES's in A10 then the possibility of autistic traits is raised.

One or more 'YES's in A9 would indicate a tic disorder. Many children go through a 'normal' developmental stage when they may blink or grimace particularly when tired or stressed. If both motor and vocal tics are present for more than 12 months then a diagnosis of Tourette's syndrome may then be considered. Tics are often associated with OCD traits and so you may find you have two or more 'YES's in A8 and A9.

Two or more 'YES's in A10 raise the probability of autistic traits being present (not necessarily autism).

Two or more 'YES's in A11/12 would again increase the probability of there being a developmental delay.

Two or more 'YES's in A13, particularly if there were two or more 'YES's in A7 would suggest that your child's diet may be having an effect upon their behaviour and this will need to be addressed.

Two or more 'YES's in A14/15 would suggest that you are losing control of your child and that immediate steps need to be taken.

The B's

It was once thought that ADHD was a self-limiting disorder that would miraculously disappear with the onset of the 3rd puberty in boys. Now we know that this is not true and untreated it can continue into adulthood carrying with it an array of problems that may cause upsets with personal relationships, difficulties within the family and even brushes with the law. As ADD / ADHD are comorbid with so many of the other learning and behavioural problems, it is essential to identify any traits or full-blown conditions in the adult members of the family.

Two or more 'YES's in B1/2 would suggest a probability of there having been a developmental delay. Two or more 'YES's in B3 would suggest aspects of dyspraxia. Two or more 'YES's in B4 would indicate that ADD / ADHD traits at least are present.

One or more 'YES's in B5 would suggest that you may have had a tic disorder or that you still have one, which may raise the probability of one of your children having a tic disorder.

One or more 'YES's in B6 would indicate that the right side of the brain is not functioning quite as it should. If your obsessions are intruding into the functioning of your daily life, you may need to seek professional advice.

If you have 'YES's for two or more questions in B7/8 it is likely that you are not functioning at your optimum level and again, may need to seek professional advice or contact Alcoholics Anonymous or Gamblers Anonymous.

<u>The C's</u>

Some of the stressors that will impact upon family dynamics can be identified and fixed with just a little of self control. Others will require a determined effort, while others – the house is too small – need a win on the lottery. However, before considering what we can do to make things better we need to identify patterns of problems within the family.

The most common stressors are 1) poverty, 2) sexual incompatibility, 3) lack of communication and 4) a problem child.

If you have one or more 'YES's in C1 then the chances are that you are stuck in a situation from which it is all but impossible to escape from. However, if we can identify other stressors that can be addressed then life can at least become more tolerable and the family has a chance of functioning at a higher level. Noise pollution is something that needs to be addressed at the earliest opportunity and will probably involve calling in the local authority.

Two or more 'YES's in C2/3 probably means your relationship is a little rocky to say the least and will require some serious soul searching as nagging doubts and jealousy means that the very foundations upon which your relationship is built are crumbling. If things are going to go horribly wrong it is best to deal with it sooner rather than later when you have no control over the outcome.

If you have two or more 'YES's in C4 you may need to take a long hard look in the mirror to see if perhaps you too have put on a few pounds or look a mess. If you don't like what you see, put it right before insisting that your partner shows you more respect. It is a great mistake to take your partner for granted and to assume that you don't have to make an effort any longer.

During courtship and the early stages of a relationship/marriage sex tends to be important to both partners and in many ways is a deciding factor in proceeding from dating to living together. If once the relationship is established and particularly children have arrived on the scene, one partner decides to change the ground-rules regarding the quality or quantity or sex, then it can be viewed as a breach of contract and this can lead to rows and a great deal of tension.

Two or more 'YES's in C6 may mean that you need to go back to the B section and check the number of ticks. Are you in the wrong job or are you carrying over from childhood problems that are colouring your personality?

Two or more 'YES's in C7 means you need to sit down while you are away from home and try to identify just what it is that is causing the problem. Are you married to the wrong person or is family life not what you expected? Whatever it is you need to be honest with yourself before you can be honest with your partner.

If there are multiple 'YES's in C8/9 you have a real problem, your marriage is not working and potentially you are harming your children. The developing brain needs love more than anything and growing up in a war zone where love is replaced with hatred is not conducive to healthy brain growth. You are the role models for your children and therefore have to present a loving, caring relationship for them to model their future relationships upon. If you swear or if the children witness violence they may assume that this is acceptable behaviour or you may drive them away if they find the situation intolerable.

Two or more 'YES's in C10 mean that you need help in deciding upon how to discipline and socially educate your children.

Multiple 'YES's in C11/12 mean that there are possible imbalances in the relationship that need to be addressed.

Two or more 'YES's in C13 simply mean that there is a breakdown in communications that needs to be addressed. Honesty in this situation is certainly the best policy and a trouble shared may indeed be a problem halved or solved.

Multiple 'YES's in C14/15/16 mean that you are losing or have lost control of your family. Steps need to be taken now before things are taken out of your hands.

Two or more 'YES's in C17 is a further sign that the dynamics of the relationship are under stress and frankly are not working.

Hopefully, by going through the process of ticking boxes above you will have identified where the problems lie or at least will have been provoked into asking questions that should have been asked a long time ago. In the following chapters we will look at what can be done to help the child/children of the relationship, the partners and thereby the family.

11 SPOT THE DIFFERENCE

Fixing the child

It may seem odd but the first step in addressing any learning or behavioural problems you may have identified in your child/children is to look at their diet. We are what we eat and your children's behaviour will reflect their intake of sugars and chemicals. Therefore, we need to look at what the family is consuming, where they eat and when they eat.

If your child has autistic traits or is on the autistic spectrum, you may have already considered trying a gluten and casein free diet. Setting up such a diet is not easy and shopping for gluten free products can be a nightmare although some supermarkets are now providing a good range of products. Rosemary Kessick's excellent book Autism & Diet is not only a very good starting point if you are planning on starting an exclusion diet but also contains some very good advice concerning certain fruits that you would be quite right in thinking were very good for you. Some children, for instance, react badly to oranges and in some cases this can trigger bed-wetting.

Here we will concentrate on establishing a healthy diet that the entire family can embrace and that will not only help every child's brain to develop as it should but will also help to alleviate the symptoms of the majority of learning and behavioural problems when accompanied by a few other changes. The diet is designed to ensure that all the dietary requirements are met, that the fuel is delivered at regular intervals and that there are no excesses in terms of sugars, salt or chemicals. Put simply, the diet should ensure that the body and brain receives everything it needs to grow and function normally, while excluding as far as possible, substances that may hinder or harm the growth and development, and where necessary, will include supplementation with essential dietary requirements.

Breakfast :	cooked not cereals
Snack:	fruit
Lunch:	packed lunch or school dinner
Snack:	fruit or carrot sticks and dips
Evening meal:	home cooked from scratch
To drink:	water, milk or diluted real fruit juice

Breakfast is where we literally break the fast and as there will have been a gap of at least 12 hours since the last meal, needs to be based on proteins, fats and carbohydrates, and not cereals or toast. Cereals may be high in sugars and salt and will be digested too easily and quickly. Therefore, the day should start with a cooked breakfast regardless of any protestations from the younger members of the family. It is a good idea to establish a two week breakfast menu so that you know what you have to prepare each morning and thus avoid getting into a rut. It is also important to think outside the box and not to limit foods to what would be considered as being a traditional breakfast. Breakfast should not be limited to scrambled eggs on toast and may include home-made fish cakes or rissoles.

A good breakfast should keep the digestive system busy for quite a while, while cereals and toast will have the brain calling for more in no time at all. Not only do we need to keep the digestive system ticking over, it is essential to drip-feed sugars into the bloodstream and to avoid at all costs sudden influxes of sugar which the brain might love but your pancreas will not be too pleased with. With childhood obesity on the increase together with rising levels of diabetes and heart disease, we have to ensure that we are not killing our children with kindness.

The mid morning snack should be some fruit and ideally fruit that you could grow in your own garden should you so desire. The logic behind this is that the more exotic the fruit, the more likely the sugar content will be higher and again here we are striving to achieve a steady blood-sugar level. The old adage 'An apple a day keeps the doctor away' comes into its own here and after all an apple not only provides a little sugar pick-me-up but also contributes to the five a day for fruit and veg.

During term time most children will have a school dinner or a packed lunch. For those that go home for lunch it is essential to keep to the balanced diet and to provide perhaps a salad during the summer or a wholesome home-made soup during autumn and winter. The packed lunch should contain a sandwich containing protein – meat or fish – some raw veg and a piece of fruit. There should be no need to include biscuits, cakes, sweets or chocolate. At no time should you offer or allow your child to have fizzy drinks. If your child is having school dinners, you may need to speak to the catering staff particularly if your child has a behavioural disorder to ensure he/she is not pigging-out on carbs.

On the way home in the car or once home, you should provide more fruit or something like carrot sticks and dips. This should be more than sufficient to keep the digestive system and brain happy until the last meal of the day is prepared. Sweets, chocolates and crisps should be treats and must not be offered or be available 24/7. Treats should be limited to twice a week and on special occasions like family days out and should be chosen carefully to exclude bad e numbers, high sugar contents and artificial sweeteners.

The evening meal should be later in the day and not when the children have just got in, thus effectively shortening the fast during the night. It should be home cooked and prepared from scratch using as far as possible fresh, wholesome ingredients. The evening meal should be a time when the family meet, greet and eat. Providing separate meals for each child is a recipe for disaster and should not be considered. The family should sit down and eat together so that the children are privy to what has been going on during the day and the parents can monitor what has been happening in school.

Limit:

- Sweets
- Chocolate
- Crisps
- Biscuits
- Cakes

Avoid:

- Fizzy drinks
- Bad E-numbers
- Artificial sweeteners
- Bad fats
- Too many carbs

Essential dietary supplements

The chances are that your child's diet will be deficient in at least omega-3 and most children with learning and behavioural disorders will benefit from added vitamins C and B complex, zinc and magnesium. Something like 60% of your brain is fat and of that fat 20% has to be the essential fatty acids. They are called essential because that is what they are and the brain cannot grow and develop properly without them. Omegas for children are readily available in pharmacies and health food shops but you will need to check the labels very carefully to make sure that they do not contain artificial colourings or sweeteners.

All supplements have to be given in age appropriate doses and this can present real problems as many of the products designed for children contain the chemicals mentioned above. To take an adult dose of vitamins and/or minerals you have to be 12 years of age, therefore for younger children you will need to source such products as Kindervital (vitamins) and Floradix Saludynam (minerals) which are additive free and can be given in age appropriate doses. Some children are also deficient in iron but before supplementing this you should see your GP.

Daily supplements:

- Omega-3 and 6 – a double dose for the first three months
- Vitamins C and B complex
- Zinc
- Magnesium

If you have any doubts that diet can influence behaviour watch any of the Super Nanny series or Tanya Byron's The House of Tiny Terrors and instead of watching the children note what they are eating, what's in the kitchen and what's in the cupboards. If your child or children are running riot address their diet before doing anything else. Two weeks of hell will quickly be replaced with calm and parental control.

Exercise

All children need general exercise in order to grow and develop normally, to develop new physical skills and to keep fit. The ever increasing number of children that are overweight or clinically obese is not just about diet but is also down to lifestyle and a serious decline in physical activity. Although the majority of children will be given physical education and sport in school, it is also necessary to provide the opportunity for children to get involved in sport and general physical activity outside of school. This provides a great opportunity for parents to become involved and is a brilliant way to establish and maintain bonding within the family.

Once a child becomes overweight and unfit, it is difficult to motivate them to take exercise and we end up with a Catch 22 position. Therefore, if you suspect that your child or children are overweight, go online and do a Body Mass Index

(BMI). This will not only put your mind at rest or confirm your suspicions but will also provide targets to work towards. Once the target is known it will require a closely monitored calorie controlled diet and a structure programme of exercises to reach the goal weight. Children that are clinically obese may require further help and expert advice should be taken.

Children that have struggled to gain good muscle tone, coordination and balance, and as a consequence, can be clumsy, accident prone and demonstrate poor spatial awareness may need specific exercises that will challenge the cerebellum. If there were quite a few ticks in A3 and A6 your child may be exhibiting dyspraxic tendencies that will need to be addressed before considering any associated learning difficulties. A list of simple tests you can carry out at home and a description of some basic exercises designed to challenge the cerebellum are contained in Appendix 1.

Reading between the lines

It has been suggested that more than 30% of children diagnosed as being dyslexic have an easily identifiable and treatable eye condition. Convergence insufficiency is the inability to bring the eyes in towards the nose smoothly and accurately, so that both eyes are looking at the same target. A failure to do this will make smooth tracking and thereby reading fluency very difficult to achieve and therefore the child will struggle to read and most likely avoid reading, which may be interpreted incorrectly as being dyslexia. A very simple test can identify that this may be the case and if this is the situation a computer generated eye test can confirm and measure accurately the nature and degree of the problem.

The Convergence Test

Sit facing your child and bringing an object - a pencil with a little animal on the end – in towards the nose from a distance of about 16".

Ask the child to keep looking at the end of the pencil while you bring it in to within 3" of the nose and back again.

Repeat this at least three times.

Try to look at both eyes at the same time and note what they do.

Results:

1) Both eyes move in together smoothly and maintain gaze on the target.

2) Both eyes move off to the side – poor visual fixation see below.

3) One eye – usually the left is slower to move in or glitches.

4) Both eyes move in and then one eye – usually the left fails to hold position.

Result 1 is normal, 2 suggests that one side of the brain is dominating – usually the left – and results 3/4 suggest that convergence insufficiency or failure are present. If convergence insufficiency is suspected then the child should be given a Visual Therapy Assessment (VTA) or Binocular Visual Assessment (BVA). If convergence insufficiency is confirmed by the VTA/BVA test, the impact it is having upon the child's ability to read can be assessed and demonstrated by carrying out a Visagraph where the number of stops and eye movements right to left are counted.

Convergence insufficiency can be treated successfully at home in a matter of weeks by using a computer generated treatment program that trains the eyes to have both slow and fast movements while in convergence but more importantly establishes accurate convergence/divergence by means of 3D images. The child's progress can be monitored by retesting using the VTA/BVA and once corrected a second Visagraph can be performed. If smooth tracking is still a problem, a computer generated treatment called Reading Plus or Dynamic Reader can be put in place to achieve reading fluency. It is not unusual for children with this problem to gain two years in their reading age in less than six months.

And so to bed

Children require a great deal of sleep and this is often far more than some parents imagine. It is essential that the child has adequate sleep not only for the brain to function correctly but also so that they are rested and ready for another day in school. If you think that sleep is not important, remember that sleep deprivation is an established interrogation technique and if you don't believe that insufficient sleep will impact upon learning, ask a school teacher if they have ever had a child drift off to sleep. You can't learn effectively when you are half asleep.

Bedtimes need to be fairly rigid and should follow a set routine so that the child can wind down in advance and look forward to their bath and bedtime story. Children that have aspects of developmental delay may establish their own routines but every child will benefit from a bedtime routine that can be followed even when away from home. Many children are afraid of the dark and if this is the case there is nothing wrong with providing a night light in the room as well as a light on the landing in case the child needs the loo or an emergency occurs.

Bedtime routine:

- Wind down time – something quiet and relaxing e.g. a puzzle or reading
- Bath time – again this should be kept quiet and relaxing
- Towelling down and into night wear
- Into bed, story, kisses and cuddles
- Leave the room and do not return

Setting boundaries – the daily routine

Children in general do better when they have a structured day and for children with any learning or behavioural problems this becomes essential. Some parents' notice that their children tend to behave better while in school than they do at home and this is because the day at school has to be structured in order that discipline can be maintained and a suitable level of calm achieved for learning to take place. A home that lacks structure and established boundaries of behaviour is a potential breeding ground for mayhem.

To live in society we have to abide by the established codes of conduct and laws of the land. Many of these rules we learn and stick to without realising, having adopted the majority of them in childhood simply because mum or dad said "We don't do that". Therefore, it is in the home and with our families that we learn to live in society. If this teaching does not take place the family will suffer and potentially society will suffer as a consequence. Boundaries and setting the basic standards of decency requires attention to physical activity, as well as verbal control and the avoidance of deviance.

Boundaries

Physical:

- Level of activity – not too over the top
- Nature of activity – must be appropriate
- Controlling the level – must not be too violent
- Observing personal space
- Only touching appropriately
- Should be age appropriate
- Must be tempered to the situation
- Must not be crude or vulgar

Verbal:

- Must learn when to speak – should not interrupt or interject
- Must not be childish or immature
- Must not be crude or vulgar
- Must not swear
- Must think before speaking
- Must not talk as a means of attracting attention to themselves

Deviance:

- A child must not be allowed to manipulate situations
- Lying is not acceptable under any circumstances
- Stealing is not permitted

- Hurting or harming animals and plants is not acceptable
- Causing another human to suffer is not permissible – bullying, etc

With most children it is only necessary to set the rules and control behaviour with simple verbal instructions, though at times the message may require an angry mummy or alpha male to deliver it for the child to respond. Discipline is the difference between a child stopping when told or running towards a busy road and potentially becoming a statistic for traffic accidents. Some children take longer to learn the ropes and others seem incapable of learning. Particularly with children that are active at the best of times and hyper at others, it will be necessary to implement a strict diet but may also be necessary to put in place measures such as the 'naughty step'. The area of the brain that is the principle site of attention deficit and hyperactivity is also the area that is involved in error correction and therefore firmer measures may be called for to increase the functioning of this area and to help it to learn by its mistakes.

Time-out on the naughty step

The naughty step should be a place where effectively the child is left on their own and where other siblings won't taunt them or have visual contact. Before placing the child on the naughty step, go down to their level so that you have eye contact and explain simply what they have done wrong. Do not engage them in conversation and place them on the step or chair where they must remain for a set period of time. The timing is based on a minute for each year of their age. Leaving the step, screaming or even speaking, means that the time-out has to be started afresh. When the time is up the child is invited to leave the step, whereupon they must say sorry for what they have done. That is, the child must state that they are sorry for doing whatever they did, so that they realise why the punishment was put in place. Once this is done a hug is in order and the matter is forgotten.

The single mother

Being a single mother can present a whole spectrum of problems but the two most common issues are guilt and the lack of an alpha male. Guilt may be too harsher word to use but often the single mother has serious concerns about the fact that there is no father. Sometimes this leads to the child being over indulged and can be used as an excuse for allowing totally unacceptable behaviour. At the risk of being labelled a male chauvinist, I would suggest that the male of the species does have a significant role to play in the upbringing of children and that instilling discipline, particularly in a young boy, is something that the male does better.

If the single mother is struggling to maintain control it is essential to ask for help long before any oppositional behaviour is established. Ideally this should be a relative but if all else fails a close and willing male friend that the child may admire will suffice. Sometimes all that is required is a role model but at other times some very obvious male disapproval may be required. This should never be of a violent nature but it should allow the child to see that a much bigger male is angry with them and does not approve of their behaviour. Once a bond is established, the 'father figure' should have a quiet chat with the child to set out the ground rules and to make clear that certain behaviour – hitting mummy – is not acceptable.

One thing all mothers need to do is teach their child/children to cook and no more is this important than with the male members of the single parent family. One it is a very important skill to have, plus it is a very good bonding tool and it is something a lot of boys find to their surprise they are very good at.

Coping with a child with OCD / Tic disorder

Adopting the diet and addressing the comorbid symptoms of OCD/Tic disorder will greatly reduce the severity of symptoms and if needs be further help can be provided at a Tinsley House Treatment Centre. However, on a day to day basis it is often necessary to cope with mood swings and emotional outbursts. As stated earlier everything that is happening in your body has to be blended with all sensory information entering your brain in the posterior insular before being passed forward to the middle insular to have the emotional component added. Having coped all day with obsessive thoughts or attempting to suppress tics, it is hardly surprising that at times the emotional centres cannot cope and all hell breaks loose.

First and foremost in this situation a great deal of understanding is required and realising just what is going on in your child's head should help you to cope and provide the appropriate response. Getting angry or telling the child off will only serve to add to the child's emotional turmoil and guilt they may be feeling. Sympathy together with an empathy borne of the knowledge of what they are going through will allow you to support the child and give them the love they so desperately need.

12 FIXING THE PARENT

Having gone through section B of the check list in chapter ten, it should now be clear if one or both adult members of the family have a problem. You do not have to have full-blown adult ADHD or OCD to consider that you might have a problem as sub clinical forms of all the learning and behavioural disabilities exist or it may be that you slipped through the net and just have not been diagnosed as having a specific aspect of developmental delay. In either case, it is only a matter of being honest with yourself and if the ticks are there consider that it just may be possible that you are causing a little disharmony in the working of the family.

As with the children of the family, the starting point is going to be looking at the diet and considering if taking supplements might help. In terms of diet, in many ways adults are harder to advise as they usually have endless reasons as to why they cannot comply with the dietary regime and are forced to eat junk food throughout the day. Most of us have to get up in the morning and head off to work but for some this is provided as an excuse as to why they cannot have breakfast. As stated above, breakfast is the most important meal of the day and should be partaken of whenever possible. Therefore, it is only necessary to adjust the alarm clock to allow the time necessary to prepare and eat a cooked breakfast.

Adults, as opposed to young children, tend to consume fairly frequent cups of tea or coffee often accompanied by a biscuit or a little treat. Do be aware that both tea and coffee contain variable amounts of caffeine – a stimulant – and that apart from piling on the calories, many snacks contain fats, sugars, salt and chemical additives. Fizzy drinks should be a definite no-no, as many contain large quantities of sugar, caffeine and artificial sweeteners and your dentist might not be too happy with you. Someone once said of alcohol that you drink the first glass, the second glass drinks the first and the third glass drinks you. I am not quite sure what that means other than all things in moderation. If you or your partner believes you have a problem, speak to the experts at AA as there is no better judge of an alcoholic than an alcoholic and remember alcoholism is a medical condition and not a social disease.

Time should be taken for a light lunch and whenever possible proceeded by some form of gentle exercise. Gaining weight, being overweight and putting yourself in line for a heart attack potentially will cause your family a great deal of heartache and suffering. During the afternoon if you are peckish have a piece of fruit and if commuting by train avoid visiting the bar or joining one of the social groups that start on the hard-stuff as the train pulls out of the station.

Stopping off at the pub on the way home or slipping out after the evening meal may be very sociable for you but is antisocial behaviour as far as the family is concerned. The evening meal should be home cooked and prepared from scratch using fresh ingredients. As far as possible the evening meal should be a family event – to meet, greet and eat together – and should take place at the dining table. It is a very important time for the children to see and speak to daddy and for daddy to cast a disapproving eye over any developing bad behaviour. Even posh families with nannies or au pairs must ensure that the children are not excluded and have ample opportunity to engage in this simplest of social activity.

A real tonic

We have talked already about the need for supplementation with omega 3 for children but do adults need to consider supplementing their diet with the omegas, vitamins and minerals? You could argue that if you are having a healthy well balanced diet that you do not need to add relatively expensive supplements which in turn provides very expensive urine and that many people's diets may well be flooded with omega 6 already but what about omega 3? The Mental Health Foundation, a group of very serious scientists, have suggested that many conditions in adults including depression, ADHD, schizophrenia and Alzheimer's may be due in part to an inadequate intake in our diet of particularly omega 3.

A great deal of research around the world has found that the cascade in the metabolism of the omegas is dependent upon other dietary factors and it has been suggested that both zinc and magnesium deficiency may influence the efficiency of the necessary breakdown, as may vitamin C and B complex if depleted. As 60% of the brain is made up of fat and 20% of the fat should be essential fatty acids, then it follows that a dietary deficiency of essential fatty acids and/or vitamins and minerals could lead to reduced brain functioning and the inability of the brain to carry out routine day to day running repairs and maintenance.

A visit to a pharmacy or health food shop will provide a selection of products that the adult can take without worrying that they may contain colourants and artificial sweeteners. When starting to take omega 3-6 it is recommended that you take a double dose for the first three months and a single dose thereafter. The vitamins and minerals taken should not exceed the recommended daily allowance.

A weight off my mind

It is not just our children that we need to keep an eye on as far as weight is concerned but for adults it can be a very touchy subject that needs to be approached with great tact and diplomacy. The best person to tell you that you have piled on a few pounds is yourself, as no matter how tactful your partner is, it will be taken as a derogatory comment indicating that you are no longer attractive. Therefore, if after having the children you have put on a bit of weight, your diet has gone to pot or hubby is developing a beer gut, now is the time to do something about it. Getting into a rut is all too easy and getting out of it tough but it can be done once you identify that you have a problem and summon up the will power to do something about it.

If it is just a matter of a few pounds, taking the dog out for an extra brisk walk may be all you need to get you back in shape. If you don't have a dog or it is a little more than a couple of pounds you need to be rid of there are organisations where you can sign up to do sponsored activities. As these activities will usually require you to be considerably fitter and lighter than you are now, you can kill two birds with one stone and shed several pounds and donate a large sum of money to your favourite charity at the same time. If you are seriously overweight you may need to consider getting professional help or registering with an organisation such as Weight Watchers.

Once you have lost weight it is important to keep up some form of regular exercise so that you don't backslide and end up where you were. And it is not just the parents that have put on a few pounds that need to exercise regularly, as apart from heart disease there are other conditions that you can help to avoid and you do need to play alongside your children. Therefore, time should be set aside during the week for personal exercise and at weekends for organised family events.

Exercise planner:

- Walking the kids to school
- Walking to work or the station
- Walking the dog
- Going for a brisk walk during the lunch break
- Going to the gym
- Going swimming
- Going to the park
- Bike riding at the weekend
- Country walk at the weekend
- Dancing
- Gardening
- Sport – football, tennis, hockey, netball, rounders, etc.
- Trampolining

From the above list select at least one thing you can do on a daily basis and two things you can do on a weekly basis.

If you ticked two or more boxes in B2/3, it may well be that you would benefit from following the exercise regime outlined in Appendix 1. Dyspraxia can take many forms and can vary in the severity from being hardly noticeable to being an accident waiting to happen. As it has the highest rate of comorbidity of all the learning and behavioural problems, the chances are that it is not the only problem you may have and together they may be having an adverse affect upon your career and family life. If you were rubbish at sports when you where a child, the chances are that you will not readily engage in sporting activities now to the detriment of your children. Being clumsy, ungainly or accident prone can make it hard to feel good about yourself and over time can dent the ego. If you feel that you may be dyspraxic you owe it to yourself and your family to do something about it.

Mind alive

Many women complain that their memory is not what it used to be following childbirth and motherhood, and a great many people have real concerns about memory loss. Dementia and Alzheimer's have received a great deal of publicity of late and you could be forgiven for thinking you are heading down that route. However, if you think of the brain as a muscle, it becomes pretty obvious that if it is not exercised it will become a bit flabby and not function too well. We are all familiar with having gone upstairs to collect something only to have forgotten what it was by the time we get there or have a word on the tip of our tongue that just won't come to mind.

If you think about it, we spend most of our young lives learning things which involves a lot of mental activity and this is usually followed by getting a job or entering a career which again provides continuing challenges for the brain. A sudden cessation of mental activity or a gradual decline can lead to the brain becoming very unfit and sluggish. The end stage of treating children with learning disabilities involves in many cases stimulating the brain with set challenges designed initially to improve processing speed, short-term memory and the ability to remain mentally focused. This works very well with children but is just as successful with the adult brain. Therefore, it is important to engage in some form of mental challenge on a daily basis.

Brain exercises

- Crossword puzzles – harder the better
- Sudoku
- Nintendo brain games
- Write a novel
- Register for Lumosity – online brain training
- Learn a foreign language
- Enrol in further education

Addressing specific issues:

OCD/Tics

If you have OCD you will be well aware of it and if it is intruding into your daily life you should seek help. Many sufferers have found great benefit just by following the simple advice given here regarding diet, supplements and exercise, but for others further treatment may be required. Being ashamed of your thoughts and not confiding in a loved one will only serve to make the guilt worse and the thoughts more intrusive. If having followed the advice provided here you do not notice a marked improvement, contact a THTC or your GP for further advice and help.

Again, if you have a full-blown tic disorder you will be very aware of the problem but many people put up with minor tics on a daily basis. Subtle facial motor tics particularly when you are tired or stressed should alert you to the need to do something about it as it is a sign that all is not well deep inside the brain. Addressing the tics may also help to improve other mental functions and should leave you feeling a lot happier. Diet and supplementation should be addressed firstly, before following the specific exercises outlined in Appendix 1. Often giving the brain what it needs and taking out of the diet substances that may potentially irritate the brain is enough to see a reduction in minor tics but for some sufferers it is necessary to follow a more advanced form of treatment and advice should be sought if symptoms persist.

Addiction – alcohol/drugs/gambling/computer games – virtual reality

If you think you may be addicted to alcohol, you are using a lot of recreational drugs or worse, your gambling has got out of control you must seek professional help. Drink and drugs will not only damage your body and brain but will also almost certainly harm your family. Not only is a drunk a poor role model but is also a parasite draining money from the family coffers. Similarly gambling, which may have started as just a bit of fun can get out of hand and take money from the family which they can ill afford to lose.

Computer games can be fun, entertaining and even therapeutic but if used excessively can become addictive. Many children that cannot concentrate for more than a few seconds will play computer games for hours totally focused on what they are doing. This is not only a problem with children and many adults will play for hours, striving to reach the next level of the game and even staying up all night in the process. It is essential to limit the time children spend playing computer games to a maximum of 30 minutes as there is a distinct possibility of an obsessive trait developing. If your partner spends endless hours gaming, it might be time to have a quiet word as not only is it possibly detrimental to their mental health, it is also not doing your marriage a lot of good.

Some computer games allow you to enter a private world where you can do pretty much as you like, including theft and even murder. One of the concerns regarding the development of virtual reality computer games, that psychologists are taking very seriously, is the often lawless nature of such games and the fact that you can be omnipotent. If you can be handsome, rich and totally powerful in your virtual world and can steal, rape and murder without any personal risk, why would you want to return to being the real you? Excessive use of computer games, even at today's level of realism, may be viewed as a form of escapism and may be a sign that the user is unhappy with their lot or that the marriage is not working.

Aggression – verbal/physical – male and female bullying at work or in the home

Verbal aggression within a relationship may be telling you that your partner has an ongoing problem, in which case you may well have married the wrong person or if it is something new, that the relationship is breaking down. In a quiet moment it is worth trying to talk it through but if that fails you may need to consider Marriage Counselling before things escalate. Physical aggression from either partner cannot be tolerated and must be dealt with immediately. Initially you must withdraw from the situation and seek professional and/or legal help. Remember, no matter what excuses you may put in place to explain the violent outburst, it should be telling you that the potential for further violence is there.

We tend to think that bullying is something that happens to young children but the facts are that it also happens to adolescents and adults. Teenage boys that are bullied tend to turn to the solace of alcohol, while teenage girls have a tendency to become violent themselves. Bullying in the workplace is common and has been cited as the most common underlying cause of absenteeism. Fortunately, in most cases bullying of this type can be dealt with effectively providing you have the courage to do something about it. Rather than bottling up all your anger, it is best to talk it over with your partner or a close friend and get them to come with you to the Personnel Department to provide the moral support you may need to see it through.

Bullying in the home is also a fairly common occurrence and is a tricky thing to deal with. The fact that you are being bullied and dominated by the very person you need to talk to about it means that you will have to use a third party and this person ideally should be of the same sex as the offender. As the bullying may well be associated with other problems, these will need to be identified and treated. If the bullying is running in parallel with a drink problem, contact AA for advice or if you suspect that your partner may have a health issue speak with your GP.

Sex

Orgasm is a right brain event and is very good for you. Apart from being very enjoyable and very relaxing, it is also one of the best ways to top up your oxytocin levels and thereby strengthen the bond with your partner.

Reasons for having sex:

- Making babies
- Bonding
- Making love
- Having fun
- Mental and physical relaxation
- Fantasising
- Giving / receiving pleasure

The most obvious reason for having sex is to make babies and thereby take the first step towards genetic immortality. When we are young we are programmed to want sex and certainly young men seem to think about it a great deal. Unfortunately, for some women once they have down their bit and produced one or two children, a hormonal switch can be thrown which causes them to go off sex. If, as is the case with some women, they have rarely attained orgasm and/or their partner is a lousy lover or a selfish person, a nice cup of tea may seem a far better choice than the whole rigmarole of getting undressed and assuming the missionary position for three minutes. Sex is something that a lot of people find difficult to talk about and yet is probably the biggest cause of marital disputes. Frankly, if you are not getting enough sex or the sex you are having is not causing the earth to move, you need to talk.

Another common reason for sex grinding to a halt after the obligatory two children is that having put up with sex as a means to an end, old demons start to rise up and sex becomes dirty, unpleasant or disgusting. It may be that as a young child you were told repeatedly that sex is dirty and is something that only bad girls do or you may have been forced into a sexual act that you found frightening or unpleasant or you may have been abused or raped. Again, if you can, talk about it with your partner or seek professional help. Some things can be so traumatic that they are repressed and become buried deep in your unconscious mind but even though the events aren't haunting you on a daily basis, they may well be driving a wedge between you and your partner which can bring about the demise of the family. Remember, your partner was not party to the events that have hurt you and cannot understand your behaviour unless you let him in. Sometimes in this situation the woman will project her guilt upon her partner blaming him for her inability to relax and enjoy some real intimacy. If you feel you can't talk to your partner, you must seek help from a professional before things go pear shaped.

Having sex on a Friday night with the lights out is a recipe for disaster, particularly if you are conscious of the fact that the children may hear your cries to god of your imminent arrival. To avoid sexual boredom may involve grasping the moment or careful planning so that you can take advantage of times that you know the children will be out or arrange for them to stay with relatives or friends. Surprising your husband with a little sexual treat in the potting shed or a quickie in the back of the car on the way home from a night out will do wonders for your marriage and rekindle the excitement you felt when you were first together (NB. It is an offence to commit a sexual act in a public place so make sure you are not caught).

We have already talked about putting on weight but those extra pounds together with not taking a pride in your appearance and poor personal hygiene is a sure way to turn your partner off, slowly but surely. Sex is a very intimate business and therefore body odour, a beer gut and soiled underwear can prove to be the best contraceptive on the planet. Taking a pride in your appearance and taking regular showers shows respect for yourself and your partner, and if you are hoping to engage in some serious foreplay it is essential.

Another fairly common cause of marital and sexual disharmony is the inability, rightly or wrongly, for a partner to forgive a past affair, a one night stand or a cutting remark or insult that occurred long ago during a row or when the partner was drunk. In this situation, unless the situation is resolved it will fester and destroy the very fabric of the family structure. Sometimes it is necessary to bite the bullet and put an end to a relationship if it cannot be repaired as at the end of the day it is the children of the marriage that must always be considered first and the trauma of a divorce may be less harmful to them than years of living in a war zone. Although love can conquer all, it must be remembered that hatred can also be contagious.

Reasons for not having sex:

- Hormonally switched off
- Sex should be just for making babies and is dirty
- Boredom
- You don't fancy him/her anymore
- You can't forgive an affair or insult
- You find certain acts repulsive or painful
- Impotency / frigidity
- No sexual honesty

Sex should be fun, relaxing and thoroughly satisfying for both partners and if there is something missing in the relationship it may only require some sexual honesty and perhaps a little Dutch courage to put things right. If you would like your wife to dress up as a nurse or god forbid a traffic warden, ask her, she may say no or you never know you could end up with a parking ticket. Bondage, S & M, role play, dressing up and sex toys could all figure in a new and exciting sex life for you and there is nothing that is wrong or perverted providing it is between consenting couples and is not dangerous. Pleasuring your partner when they are tired or when they deserve to be pampered is a great way of showing how much you care and can serve as an aperitif for things to come.

Impotence and frigidity can be a real problem for the sufferer and can impact upon the working of the marriage as one partner may be missing out on their own sexual fulfilment. Medical treatment for these conditions have greatly improved over the last few years and although highly embarrassing for you, will be met with understanding and a caring approach by your GP or specialist. Difficult or painful intercourse may only require a little lubrication but if that does not help consult your GP. Lastly, before moving on we have to consider the possibility that one of the partners has discovered that they are gay or one of your children drops, what for many parents would be a bombshell, that they are attracted to members of the same sex. If you are engaged in a homosexual relationship and particularly if you are a male, then you should come out of the closet as soon as possible and bear in mind the possibility that you may transmit a venereal disease to your partner if you are also having sex with them. Apart from acceptance, a gay child only needs the love you would bestow upon any child.

Child abuse and incest

Any hint or suggestion of mental, physical or sexual abuse of a child must be reported to the authorities immediately. We have all read in the newspapers and heard on the news about how children have suffered and died, therefore you must talk to someone that can intervene at the earliest possible time.

13 FIXING THE FAMILY

Providing you are able to fix any problems that you may have with the members of your family, it should be relatively easy to put into place strategies and activities that will help the family unit to function at a higher level. However, if you have identified any serious problems with the relationship with your partner it may well be that you have some tough times ahead or you may need to put in place a damage limitation policy to prevent, as far as possible, the children from suffering.

The kids

Before making any attempt to fix the family and addressing any imbalances in the workings and dynamics of its structure, it is necessary to be sure that each member of the family is functioning at an optimum level and that as many stressors as possible have been removed. When considering the problems children of the family may be subject to think about learning and behaviour in toddlers, schoolchildren and adolescents. In terms of the difficulty in fixing the problem in children, it is best to think in terms of levels one, two and three.

Level one can be thought of as behavioural and motor learning issues in toddlers and providing that there are no other medical conditions that could delay development, should be dealt with adequately with dietary modification, supplementation and the establishment of fixed boundaries. If after two months the regime is not working you should contact a THTC for advice.

10 Daily Strategies for coping:

1) Have a routine and stick with it

2) Remember you are the parent and in charge

3) Thinking that you are being kind (giving sweets) is not a good idea

4) Stick or carrot. Choose the most appropriate discipline technique for your child. Some kids will respond to incentives/rewards, others to punishments/loss of rewards or incentives

5) Be consistent

6) Say what you mean and mean what you say

7) Be kind but firm when necessary

8) Curb all bad behaviour from the start – if you are losing it seek help

9) Have fun with your kids / find time for them

10) Give hugs each and every day

Level two involves learning/academic and behavioural issues in schoolchildren. If your child has a problem with reading, try the simple convergence test described above. If the results don't look too promising or if you are unsure of the results contact a local optician and ask if they can do a convergence test or call a THTC for an assessment. Convergence insufficiency could be impacting upon your child's ability to read and as it can be diagnosed in minutes and treated in weeks, it would be a pity to let this potential problem go unnoticed.

If convergence insufficiency is shown to be present the use of Home Therapy System, a computer generated treatment program, should resolve the situation in a few weeks. Once the convergence insufficiency has been treated it is advisable to have a Visagraph completed to ensure that the eyes are tracking smoothly and if they are not, Reading Plus or Dynamic Reader should be started.

Many children in this category will also struggle with spellings and this can be addressed by using computer generated spelling programs such as Spellodrome, which can be purchased online. If maths is also a problem, Mathletics, another computer generated program can be purchased online. The benefit of these two programs is that they are cheap and can be set up to address the needs of all age groups of children. Once reading, spelling and maths have been attended to, it is possible to increase processing speed, attention and memory with the use of such computer programs as Lumosity, which again can be purchased online.

Behavioural issues in level two will require a little more care and attention as there will be times when you will have no control over the child's diet and consumption of banned items of food and drink plus disciplinary measures may be different or absent. It is very important that you speak to whoever is looking after your child – school, relatives or childminders – to ensure that they know what is allowed in terms of food and behaviour.

This of course also applies to toddlers in group one and particular attention needs to be paid to grandparents who may not understand what it is you are trying to achieve and may think you are just being cruel, or ex-husbands that are hellbent on throwing a spanner in the works. Either way, make sure you are in charge and also remember to monitor pocket money and your purse to ensure your child is not supplementing your carefully applied diet with sweets and fizzy pop. Even with the best will in the world it is sometimes not possible to deal with your own children particularly as a single parent and sometimes it is necessary to call in the cavalry. There is nothing wrong with this and it does not signify defeat. Quite the opposite, just like giving up on trying to teach a member of the family to drive and providing driving lessons with a professional instructor, sometimes professional help is needed.

Children and adolescents in level three may be showing signs of oppositional behaviour or even a conduct disorder in which case professional advice is essential. Older children and adolescents may/will have attained both physical size and strength, to a point where they may use it against you to get their own way. If an older child is using verbal or physical aggression towards you, you have lost respect and control and must consider seeking professional help immediately. If you have lost your position in the peckingorder there is nothing you can do about it unless miraculously you can change into a 25 stone sumo wrestler overnight and let's face it that is not going to happen.

The other half

Assuming that as far as the children are concerned all is going well, it is time to look at the other half in the relationship and also yourself. The potential problems you may have identified may be a history of learning or behavioural problems that have not been addressed, obsessive behaviour, addiction or a sociopathic disorder. Just as with the children, these issues need to be addressed and not swept under the carpet.

Learning disabilities in adults can be addressed in exactly the same ways as with children and with good compliance can be very effective. If you think you may have dyslexia there is a 30% chance that you have convergence insufficiency in which case your reading can be dramatically improved in less than six months. It is exactly the same with spelling and although it cannot be guaranteed that you will be a budding Einstein, your maths can be improved to help you cope more easily on a daily basis. Handwriting in both adults and children can be helped by learning calligraphy as this is a cross between writing and drawing and therefore uses slightly different areas of the brain.

Although clumsiness and ADHD tendencies in adults can be helped significantly by specific exercises and diet, OCD and tics may well require professional advice before an improvement can be noticed. Addiction to alcohol, drugs or gambling will require specialist help as the brain is very good at trying to fool you and let you think you can overcome the problem single-handedly. The truth of the matter is that the odds are stacked against you and you will require a helping hand. This is not an admission of failure but a positive courageous step forward that demonstrates clearly that you are bigger and better than you think you are.

Any aspects of anti-social behaviour in a partner needs very special consideration as it will potentially influence or damage the children of the relationship. Minor lapses can be dealt with in-house by a strong partner of either gender but more serious activities will require outside help.

Anti-social behaviour:

- Swearing
- Verbal aggression
- Physical aggression
- Recurrent drunkenness in the home
- Noise pollution
- Any form of child abuse
- Drunkenness in public
- Abuse of neighbours
- Fighting
- Vandalism
- Use of drugs
- Reckless/dangerous driving
- Theft
- Any criminal activity

It may be sad but in some cases it is true that you may be living with or married to the wrong person. You may have thought that you could change him/her but the old saying about leopard and spots is often correct and you may have to come to realise that having done the best you could for all the right reasons, you have failed and perhaps need to move on. Perhaps the person you fell in love with did not really exist, being no more than a figment of your imagination or was consciously deceiving you to get whatever he or she wanted. Either way, you have been duped and again need to be able to move on for the sake of the children.

This approach may seem harsh and a little bit too clinical and will surely upset the more devout reader but we do at the end of the day have to think about the product of the union and not any idealistic thoughts about how things should be. So far there has been little mention of religion as I believe it would be wrong to impose any views I may hold onto the reader and conversely it would be wrong to impose any heartfelt beliefs of your own in a world that is far from perfect or to blame another faith for the rise in anti-social behaviour. We must learn to be tolerant of others before we can be tolerant of our own imperfections.

The family: the house – rooms and their use

How the family occupy and use the various rooms of the house can give a number of clues as to how the family is functioning and an awareness of this usage can provide the means to alter the dynamic process. For instance, a computer with internet access in a child's room may cause them to become socially isolated from the family and gives them the opportunity to use the computer excessively or inappropriately. Not using the dining room at least once a day means that the family is not making the most of time together and may be a sign that the family structure is or has disintegrated.

The kitchen is the hub of most households and apart from cooking is where a great deal of social activity does or should take place. The bringing home of food and its subsequent preparation is a primitive and yet very important process in terms of survival, bonding and the setting up of the pecking order. Trekking around the supermarket may not be your idea of fun but bringing home the bacon is vital to the survival of the family in more ways than one. If you doubt for one moment that this is true think of the excessive food purchases that go on at Christmas and the panic buying associated with any mention of a food shortage. It may be painful on the purse but there is a deep subconscious satisfaction associated with stocking the cupboards and filling the fridge-freezer.

The kitchen and/or breakfast room is where not only members of the family may gather at certain times of the day but also where friends and relatives will be entertained when they drop by for a chat. It has then a functional and social usage which is underpinned by the subtle pleasures associated with the smell of meat roasting or other tummy rumbling aromas, and the knowledge that your hunger will soon be satisfied. The kitchen should also be the place where produce from the kitchen garden or a fishing trip are brought to be prepared and culinary skills are passed on to the next generation. Girls and boys should be taught at least the basic cooking skills and family recipes should be passed on, not just Delia's creations. Washing up or loading the dishwasher should be part of this learning curve.

As shopping has in most cases replaced the need for hunting and harvesting, it is only right and proper that dad should, whenever possible, do his bit in the kitchen. Apart from setting a good role model, it also provides mum with a bit of time to pamper herself or join the kids in the garden for a bit of fun before eating. Role reversal is important, as apart from giving mum a break from the kitchen chores, it also helps prevent the children from adopting stereotypes. That is, the days when certain activities in the home and in the workplace were considered as being women's work or men's work are long gone or certainly should be.

After the kitchen we must consider the dining room. This room should be used at least once a day and should be considered as being a social area and not just a functional area. Yes, we have to eat to live but eating should, as far as possible, be a time when the family come together to eat, talk, learn and have fun. Now I know you shouldn't talk with your mouth full, but in between mouthfuls is a great time to find out what the children have been up to and to plan future events.

The learning aspect that may come from dining together should not only involve answering questions the children may raise about any topic or their homework but also at least the basics of table manners if not the more formal etiquette required for more formal dining. Children have to learn to progress from finger food to the use of firstly, a spoon, and then the whole tricky business of a knife and fork. It is not a bad idea to lay the table more formally for special occasions so that when the children get older they are not going to be phased by an array of cutlery which can prove to be very embarrassing.

Once children have mastered the art of using the tools of eating, it is important to work on the speed at which the food is consumed, the need for chewing and the reduction of debris on the tablecloth. Hungry children will tend to shovel the food into their mouths and many children will swallow the mouthful as quickly as possible with a minimum of chewing. As digestion starts in the mouth it is very important to ensure that children slow down and chew their food well or indigestion may ensue later in life when the body becomes a little less tolerant of such abuse. Most children are messy eaters during their apprenticeship but if they continue to wear their food steps should be taken to direct the food to the mouth without mishaps.

Once the meal is over, the dining table provides the perfect surface and setting for board games. You might be forgiven for thinking that Monopoly is a bit old hat but such games provide a wonderful opportunity to interact with the children and also to teach them basic values such as honesty and the acceptance of losing. You are in a much better situation and position to deal with a child that loses the plot in the comfort of your own home rather than an aisle in the supermarket. Some games, such as Scattergories are actually good for the brain in that they make your brain do a little workout and are good wholesome family fun.

The sitting room, lounge, or if you are really posh, the drawing room, is a place where the family tend to spend quite a bit of time together. Unfortunately, the room is often dominated by a television which in some households tends to be on from morning until night. I am not knocking the use of the television as the various channels can provide good entertainment if you just need to chill-out and watch informative documentaries, but there should be a limit as to how much TV you and particularly the children watch. More and more these days young children are being stuck in front of the television so that mum can get on with the household chores and there is a danger that this can be the start of a very bad habit.

The television just like the computer should be used selectively and if any of your children have a tic disorder, should be limited to one programme a day. The sitting room should be a place to sit comfortably and talk or read a book as well as the ideal place to snuggle up and watch your favourite programme. It should not be exclusively a television room. With more and more families having more than one television set, there is a danger that children are being exposed to a constant bombardment of passive entertainment without which they are instantly bored. Children need to read, play games and create their own entertainment as opposed to sitting on their backsides and being encouraged to be inactive and consequently unfit.

The sitting room can also double up as a gym for such activities as yoga and for parents to challenge the youngsters to Wii Sport or Fit when the weather is inclement. There is no real substitute for getting out into the fresh air to partake of sporting activities but when, as is often the case during the winter months this is not possible, a game of tennis or golf in the sitting room can be great fun. Childhood obesity is becoming a real problem and every effort should be made to engage the children in some form of sporting activity that makes you sweat at least twice a week.

If you are lucky enough to have a study or playroom, this should be a TV free zone. It is the ideal place to situate the family computer as it is not a good idea for children to disappear off to their bedrooms where out of sight often means out of mind. Older children in particular need and deserve their privacy but this can be abused and apart from over usage of computer games, chat rooms and inappropriate sites may be secretly visited. The study should contain a selection of essential books – dictionaries, thesauruses, atlases, classics, etc. – and a work station where all members of the family may work in peace and quiet. It should be an open access room where people can come and go freely, thus limiting the opportunity to use the computer inappropriately but should operate rather like a library in terms of noise levels and disturbances.

For families with younger children, somewhere on the ground floor, there should be a place for time-out or a recognised 'naughty step'. The use of the 'naughty step' should be instigated at the first sign of any behavioural problems and must be used correctly and appropriately by the adult in charge of the children. The time-out zone or 'naughty step' must be situated so that the adult can keep an eye on the child and also ensure that any other children do not speak to or taunt the child that is being disciplined.

Sending a child to their room has the effect of isolating them from the rest of the family but also gives them the opportunity to play, use the computer or trash the room and so should not be considered as a form of punishment.

Moving upstairs there are three rooms to consider. Firstly, there is the bathroom which apart from being the centre of personal hygiene is also a great place to relax and for younger children it is a play area. Children need to be taught the essentials of personal hygiene including putting their used clothing in the washing basket, cleaning their teeth effectively, bathing or showering and washing their hair. The routines and frequency of these essentials need to be instilled at an early age as older boys in particular can become allergic to soap and water. It is very important to establish a winding-down routine where the child has their evening meal, has a short play time, has their bath, puts on their PJ's and then settles down in bed to listen to the bedtime story.

Ideally each child should have their own bedroom and this need for personal space and privacy becomes evermore important as the children get older. Expressions like "There's no place like home" basically mean that familiarity provides a feeling of security and this sense of feeling safe is very important. Children that are showing signs of developmental delay need familiarity and routines to help them feel secure and their own personalised space is essential to this. However, it is equally important to ensure that any child that is struggling does not migrate and spend too much time in their room avoiding contact with the family and thus losing interaction with its members.

Children need to have fixed bedtimes for school days, weekends and holidays. If you struggle to get the children out of bed of a morning or you get feedback from school that the child appears tired or actually falls asleep, you may need to consider revising their bedtime to ensure that they are getting adequate sleep. When there is disharmony in the family it is not unusual for one parent to allow a child or the children to stay up later with them. This is a subtle way of winning over the children as a way of getting at the partner but comes at the expense of the unwitting youngsters. Allowing the child to stay up and watch television is also something that may occur when the child is visiting their father following divorce and can be part of a package of lapses in routine designed to make life difficult for the ex partner when the child is returned.

The adult's bedroom needs to be a relatively private space into which the children have limited access. It is not a good idea to allow children to get into the habit of sharing the marital bed or feeling they can wander in at any time. Parents, like children, need personal space and the freedom to indulge in adult activities without any nagging doubts that little Mary is going to burst in because she has lost her favourite teddy. A lockable bedroom door allows adults the privacy they deserve and the psychological reassurance necessary to completely relax and enjoy adult time together. Enforced coitus interruptus, apart from being very frustrating at the time, can be a recipe for disaster if it occurs on more than one occasion.

Moving outside the house we must now consider the garden and how it can be put to various uses that will help the family to function at an optimum level. The garden should be a place where children can play safely on their own but also where the family can enjoy playing games together and, weather permitting, eat out. Depending on the size of the garden, as much equipment as possible should be provided to encourage exercise and the ability to just have fun. Again, depending upon the size of the garden it is good to involve children from an early age in the basics of gardening, particularly picking flowers for the house and growing vegetables. There is nothing more rewarding than harvesting your own produce that can be brought to the kitchen and also the knowledge that the children are learning about organic vegetables and eating them. Having grown, watered and harvested the crop, children may well be more inclined to eat their veg and to try new varieties.

If the garden is small it is essential to make good use of local parks and facilities to ensure that the children have somewhere to let off steam, have fun and get enough exercise. Children that are slow to develop or are a little nervous of play apparatus should be encouraged to use progressively more challenging and exciting slides, roundabouts and swings. If done correctly, the child will become more confident and certain areas of the brain will be stimulated and encouraged to develop. Apart from local parks and theme parks, it is also a good idea to encourage children to join clubs and organisations where they can not only exercise but learn the various disciplines involved with each activity.

The discipline that must be in place to be a Cub, Scout or Sea Cadet provides a valuable learning curve for children and may broaden their social and physical skills which in turn will increase their level of self confidence. Children with dyspraxia and in particular ADHD may benefit greatly from the discipline and acquired poise associated with the martial arts. It may seem strange to teach a child that may already be showing signs of physical aggression how to hit and kick their opponents with far greater efficiency but in fact this is not the case. A well run karate class will instil discipline from the start and the master will gain immediate respect. Donning a uniform often involves adopting the mantle of the behavioural model and can transform a naughty child into a compliant well behaved boy or girl.

Holidays, when possible, afford the family the opportunity to relax and spend time together which is not always possible at home. Also, sunshine holidays mean that days can be spent on the beach, facilities that may not be readily available at home are on hand and balmy evenings mean that the children can stay up a little later and join their parents at a local restaurant. Apart from being fun, holidays may also provide learning opportunities in terms of visiting local sites but also as an immersion into a different culture and the exposure to foreign languages. Holidays ideally should be multifaceted and not just an excuse for mum and dad to sit round the pool drinking a little more than perhaps they should as in the TV programme, Benidorm for example.

Lastly, we need to think about the school and what we need to achieve in terms of the child's education. We should want the very best for our children but not at the expense of pushing them beyond their capabilities. Children must be safe, happy and given every opportunity to reach their own particular potential. Each child will have their own unique abilities and it is the job of the parents and the educational system to find and encourage their strengths while attempting to mitigate any weaknesses.

Not every child can go to the best schools in the land, be privately educated or attend a public school and this is neither essential nor always desirable, and we have all had the experience of meeting an educated idiot. However, the school must be able to cater to the child's specific needs regardless as to whether the child is gifted or struggling. Therefore, it is incumbent upon the parents to not only research which schools are available to the child but also how the individual school can meet the needs of the child in terms of academic challenge and/or special needs provision.

Parents need to be proactive in not only finding the right school but also in closely monitoring their child's progress and intervening at an early stage if there are any doubts. If the child appears to be struggling or is unhappy it is important to have a word with their teacher to find out if anything is going on in the background or to ask for help and perhaps the need for an assessment either in school or privately. If you are actively involved in your child's education and are on the ball, the situation where you are called into the school should not occur or indeed be necessary.

PS.

There is one ingredient that is essential to the well-being of children and the success of the family unit and that is having a great sense of humour. Life should be about having as much fun as possible while still learning, earning and yearning. Therefore, it is important to embarrass your children by skipping in a public place, impressing them with your ability on the Nintendo Wii and providing each child with a family nickname. Love may conquer all but a sense of humour can brighten any day and make the journey through life far more enjoyable and successful.

APPENDIX – SPECIFIC EXERCISES

A testing time

Before attempting these specific exercises it is essential to carry out the series of simple tests that follow in order to establish which side of the body and hence the brain needs to be exercised. Following each test tick the appropriate box - Left or Right (copy the Test Box below on to a scrap of paper).

	RIGHT	LEFT
TEST 1		
TEST 2		
TEST 3		
TEST 4		
TOTAL		

TEST 1

Stand in front of a friend or your partner with your feet together, hands by your side and eyes closed. Have them gently but firmly tap your upper arm just below shoulder level, firstly on the left then on the right. Have them repeat this two or three times. Have them note if you lose balance, move a foot or an arm. Tick the box for the side that you fell towards or the opposite side to the foot or arm that moved. That is, if the right arm or foot moves you tick the left box.

TEST 2

Sit in front of your partner with your arms outstretched and the index finger of each hand pointing directly at their nose. With your eyes closed you must touch your nose and then point at their nose, firstly with the index finger of the right hand and then with the left. This should be repeated several times consecutively and must be done with the eyes closed. Have them note if one finger repeatedly misses the nose or if there is a slight hesitation before the finger touches the nose. Tick the box for the finger that repeatedly misses the target or has a slight tremor before making contact.

TEST 3

Sit in front of your partner and stretch your arms out in front of you. With your eyes open, turn your hands to the palm up position and rapidly alternate the movement palms down / palms up. Have your partner look for the hand that goes out of sync first or the elbow that bends and then tick the appropriate box.

APPENDIX – SPECIFIC EXERCISES

TEST 4

Sit facing your partner, with your elbows by your side and forearms outstretched in front of you palms upwards. Then turn your hands palm down/up as rapidly as possible while keeping your elbows by your side. Have your partner note which hand goes out of sync first or which wrist bends producing a waving movement. Tick the box as to left or right.

Now look at your TEST BOX. If three or more ticks are left or right you are safe to proceed with the following exercises. If you are unsure about any of the results or the results are evenly mixed you should consult an experienced practitioner.

The following exercises should only be started once you have completed the tests above and you are confident of the results. Here we will assume that you have ticked three or four of the LEFT boxes. If you have ticked off three or four of the RIGHT boxes then simply swap right for left in the instructions given below.

The following exercises should be carried out on a daily basis in conjunction with the progressive stair-walking exercises. You must do exercise one on a daily basis plus at least one of the other two:-

PROGRESSIVE STAIR-WALKING EXERCISE

1. With hands by the side, head in the neutral position and eyes closed, walk up and then down 3 stairs, 3 times, 3 times a day. Never go higher than 3 stairs. When you can do 3 repetitions perfectly, do 5, then 7, then 10.
2. Once you have mastered forward stair-walking, do it backwards with the same progressions.
3. Once you can stair walk forwards and backwards, start forward stair-walking again but this time carrying a tray with a plastic tumbler full of water on it.

CAUTION – When first starting the Progressive Stair-Walking Exercise have a friend or your partner close at hand in case you stumble or fall. This can be discontinued once you have progressed and feel confident to exercise alone.

DAILY LATERAL EXERCISES

1. Twice a day when cleaning your teeth – use your left hand and stand on your left leg.
2. Teach yourself to use a yo-yo using your left hand. Learn as many tricks as possible.
3. Stand on your left leg while listening to a piece of music. Conduct the orchestra with your left hand only and sing along to the music if possible (best done in private).

Once you have been doing these activities for around six weeks, do the four tests again and see if you and/or your partner see an improvement.

The physical exercises should be continued until they are perfected. If you continue to struggle with the exercises or show no sign of progress after, say, two months, consider contacting a Tinsley House Treatment Centre for advice – http://tinsleyhouseclinic.co.uk. 'Finding a clinic near you' is on the first page.

So how does it work?

The general cerebellar exercises are non-specific exercises designed to challenge the cerebellum, making the 'weaker' side come up to speed.

LEFT/RIGHT specific cerebellar exercises are designed to challenge one cerebellar hemisphere via the need to balance and/or produce novel movements.

LEFT/RIGHT specific brain exercises are designed to challenge known functions of the left/right cerebral hemispheres. To give you an example of this look at the letter T below:-

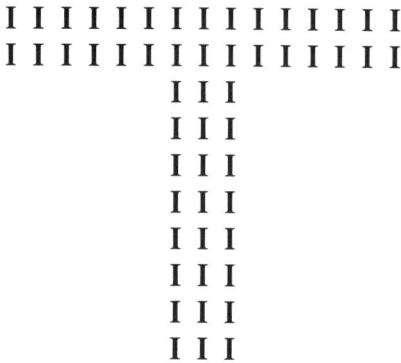

If you look at the letter 'T' from a distance you are using the right side of the brain. Once you look at the detail and see it is made up from the letter 'I' you are using the left side of the brain. The right side of the brain sees the big picture while the left side examines the detail. There are a great many functions which are specifically left/right and some which can be attributed to specific areas of the brain on one side. By knowing the sidedness of these functions it is possible to 'exercise' set areas of the brain.

A little help

Once the diet and supplementation are in place and the exercises are progressing well you are going to need a little help from a health professional if you feel that further treatment is necessary. For instance if your primary problem is with reading speed and you suspect you may have secondary dyslexia, then you will need to have certain tests carried out in a clinic or optometrists office that has the facility to carry out such testing before you can start the computer generated treatment plan. Unfortunately, all the computer generated treatment programs have to be prescribed to fit the specific needs of the individual or dispensed by an optometrist and cannot be simply purchased at PC World.

(Taken from Could It Be You? Pub. Virgin Books)

Disclaimer

The exercises and activities described above are intended to help children/adults with learning/behavioural problems. If you have any concerns about your health you should contact a health professional for advice.

FURTHER READING

Is That My Child?
The Brain Food Plan, and
Could It Be You?

by Robin Pauc. (Publisher: Virgin Books)

are available through the Amazon website.

GLOSSARY

Accommodation/convergence failure
the inability of the eyes to move in towards the nose when looking at something close up, eg when reading.

Acetylcholine
a substance used by nerves to send messages to other nerves.

Afferentating
causing messages to be sent into the nervous system.

Allo
the allocortex is a part of the cerebral cortex (outer layer of the brain) characterized by having fewer cell layers (3) than the isocortex (6).

Alpha-linolenic acid
an omega-6 essential fatty acid.

Amino acids
the 'building blocks' that make up proteins.

GLOSSARY

Anterior cingulate
the Anterior cingulate cortex (ACC) is the frontal part of the cingulate cortex, which resembles a "collar" formed around the corpus callosum (the body that joins the two cerebral hemispheres).

Antioxidants
chemical components of foods that neutralise harmful free radical molecules that damage the body's cells.

Apoptosisis
the name given to the programmed cell death that occurs during development of the brain. Cells that do not migrate or make contact with other neurons die.

Arachidonic acid
a polyunsaturated fatty acid that is essential for growth.

Archiocortex
the outer layer of the brain is called the cortex. There are three types of cortex – archio, paleo and neocortex. The first two are called primitive cortex (older) while the last type is the newest in terms of brain evolution.

Artificial sweeteners
artificially produced chemicals, many times sweeter than sugar, added to food for sweetness.

Aspartame
also known as E951: The best known (and most infamous) artificial sweetener, alleged to contribute to a variety of health problems.

Asperger's syndrome
a disorder in which the individual shows marked deficiencies in social skills, does not like change, often has obsessive routines and becomes preoccupied with particular subjects.

Attention deficit disorder (ADD)
an inability to focus/concentrate on the job in hand, with a tendency to be easily distracted – tends to go hand in hand with ADHD – it is a classic symptom of developmental delay.

Attention deficit hyperactivity disorder (ADHD)
as for ADD above but with aspects of hyperactivity and impulsivity.

Autism (true)
affects about 1 in 5000 children, being four times more common in boys than girls – it has been thought for some time to be due to abnormal brain development. Autistic children avoid eye contact, shun affection, do not understand other people's emotions/feelings, have problems making friends and cannot adjust to the rules of society.

Autistic spectrum disorder (ASD)
affects 9 in 1000 children. These children display autistic tendencies and it may well prove to be an extreme form of developmental delay due to reduced numbers of von Economo neurons (VENs) or greatly impaired development of VENs.

Azo dye
a synthetic dye, usually red, brown or yellow, which make up about half the dyes we use.

Benzoate
chemical used as a food preserver.

Blood sugar level
the amount of sugar in the blood stream at any one given moment of time.

Bpoptosis
a term coined in 2005 by R Pauc to cover the period of time during which the second-wave/generation of human

brain cells develop, migrate and make contact with other neurons.

Brainstem
the part of the nervous system that joins the brain to the spinal cord: it contains many of the vital centres – vital because without them you die.

Caffeine
stimulant chemical, found in coffee, and also tea, chocolate, energy drinks and some cold remedies.

Calories
unit of measurement for the energy found in food.

Carbohydrates
a component of food, used to produce energy in the body. Can be divided into sugary carbohydrates and starchy carbohydrates.

Carcinogen
a substance thought to cause cancer.

Central Nervous System (CNS)
the brain and spinal cord.

Cerebellar hemisphere
the cerebellum has a middle section (vermis = worm) with a large lobe on either side called a hemisphere.

Cerebellum
literally 'little brain' that lives in the very back of the skull under the brain.

Cerebral hemisphere
the name given to either side of the brain.

Cholesterol (HDL)
the 'good' kind of cholesterol that reduces your risk of clogged arteries, heart disease and stroke.

Cholesterol (LDL)
the 'bad' kind of cholesterol that increases your risk of clogged arteries, heart disease and stroke.

Chromosomal
to do with chromosomes, which are the threadlike structures found in the nucleus of cells and which carry the genes.

Comorbidity
when two or more conditions appear together at the same time.

Compliance
obeying the rules.

Congenital
present at birth.

Convergence failure
the inability to bring the eyes in towards the nose, necessary for close vision.

Corpus callosum
the body of white matter joining the two cerebral hemispheres.

Cranial Nerves
12 pairs of nerves found at the base of the brain and brainstem.

Cross Cord Reflexes
messages that get passed from one side of the spinal cord to the other so that we can do things like walking, swimming etc.

Developmental Delay Syndrome (DDS)
a slowing in the development/maturation of the brain which causes the symptoms of dyslexia, dyspraxia, attention deficit, hyperactivity, obsessions and tics to occur.

GLOSSARY

Diabetes
usually refers to diabetes mellitus, a disorder characterised by excessive urinary excretion. Common types are Type 1 juvenile diabetes, Type 2 adult diabetes and Gestational – occurring during pregnancy.

Diaschisis
put simply this is when one area of the brain does not work too well because an area it normally communicates with has a problem. So it is a bit like a couple having a row and not talking to each other.

Disaccharide
A sugar made up of two 'sugar units' joined together. Examples include sucrose (table sugar) and lactose (the sugar found in milk).

Docosahexaenoic Acid
an omega 3 essential fatty acid.

Dopamine signalling
messages sent from one nerve to another using a special substance – a neurotransmitter called dopamine.

Dressing dyspraxia
difficulty dressing.

Dysarthia
inability to produce clear speech.

Dysdiadochokinesia
the inability to make rapidly alternating movements – turning the hands palm up/down.

Dyslexia
a term used to cover a variety of learning difficulties.

Dysmetria
inaccurate movements.

Dyspraxia
an inability to perform learned movements accurately: can take many forms and has been found to be present in association with the other symptoms of developmental delay in over 90 per cent of children.

Echolalia
repeating what you have just heard.

Eicosanoids
signalling molecules, derived from omega-3 and omega-6 essential fatty acids, involved in immunity and inflammation.

Eicosapentaenoic acid
an omega -3 essential fatty acid.

Empty calories
food/calories that provide energy (and can lead to weight gain) with little or no other nutritional benefit. A label often applied to sugar!

Equasym
Equasym tablets and Equasym XL capsules both contain the active ingredient methylphenidate hydrochloride, which is a type of medicine called a stimulant. It is used to treat attention deficit hyperactivity disorder (ADHD) in children.

Flavour/flavoured (on labels)
Foods labelled 'flavour' (eg 'strawberry flavour') need not contain any of the real ingredient (in this case, strawberries) – their taste can come entirely from artificial additives. Foods labelled 'flavoured' (eg 'strawberry flavoured') must actually contain that ingredient.

GLOSSARY

Foetal Alcohol Spectrum Disorder
a fairly recent new term to cover both the physical and neurological effects to the foetus due to the maternal ingestion of alcohol during pregnancy.

Foetal distress
when the foetal heartbeat rises or drops dramatically.

Folic acid
a member of the B vitamin group, needed by pregnant women to reduce the risk of neural tube defects (such as spina bifida). Could also benefit heart health.

Functional dominance
when one area of the brain is superior or dominent in function.

Functional foods
foods which claim to have health benefits beyond normal nutrition. Many have had their nutritional properties artificially boosted, for example by the addition of 'friendly bacteria', or omega-3 essential fatty acids.

Gamma-linoleic acid
an omega-6 essential fatty acid.

Gigantopyramidal cells
very large motor neurons found in the mid cingulate gyrus (inside wall of the brain).

Glue ear
a condition when the middle ear is filled with a glue-like fluid instead of air.

Glycaemic Index (GI)
a measure of the amount that a food increases blood sugar level.

Glycaemic Load (GL)
a more sophisticated form of the Glycaemic Index, that takes into consideration the amount per serving that a food increases blood sugar level.

Hormones
a chemical messenger transported around the body in the bloodstream.

HUFAs
highly unsaturated fatty acids.

Hydrogenated fats
fats that have been artificially altered to change their hardness and increase their keeping properties. Found in many manufactured foods, they form a large proportion of the harmful 'trans' fats in our diets.

Hypothalamus
a tiny area of the brain weighing c. 4 grams that control basic functions such as hunger, thirst, oxygen levels in the blood, etc.

Interneurons
small nerves that interconnect with other nerves.

Irritable Bowel Syndrome (IBS)
a multi-faceted disorder thought to be due to a disturance in the interaction between the intestines, the brain and the autonomic nervous system, which alters the regulation of bowel function. It is characterised by abdominal pain or discomfort and is associated with a change in bowel pattern, such as loose or more frequent bowel movements, diarrhoea and/or constipation.

Linoleic acid
an omega -6 essential fatty acid.

Meconium
the first stool a baby passes.

GLOSSARY

Methylphenidate Hydrochloride
a central nervous system stimulant better known as Ritalin.

Monosaccharide
a single unit sugar, for example glucose or fructose.

Monosodiam Glutamate (MSG)
A flavour enhancer, also known as E621. Implicated in behavioural symptoms such as hyperactivity.

Monounsaturated fat
a 'healthy' kind of fat that benefits your cholesterol levels. Olive oil, and also the oils found in nuts and seeds, are good sources.

Motor planning
how the brain plans what it is it wants to do.

Motor skills
the ability to carry out physical things you have learned to do.

Myelin
the fatty insulation that covers nerve fibres.

Myelination
the process that takes place during development when certain nerves are wrapped in myelin.

Myopic
being nearsighted.

Neocortex
in terms of evolution, the newest parts of the brain.

Neuroanatomy
the anatomy of the nervous system.

Neuroepithelium
specialised tissue in the developing brain that produces firstly neurons (nerves) and then all other brain cells.

Neurologist
an expert in neurology.

Neurology
the study of the nervous system.

Neurons
nerves.

Neurotoxic
nerve poison.

Neurotransmitter
a chemical substance that passes messages from one nerve to the next.

Nystagmus
the flickering of the eyes from side to side.

Obsessive-compulsive disorder (OCD)
is characterised by a recurrent urge to carry out ritualistic behaviour patterns. It is a common symptom of developmental delay. To a certain extent we all have minor aspects of compulsive behaviour, only becoming a problem when it occurs to such a degree that it takes over a person's waking life.

Omega -3 and -6 fatty acids
forms of polyunsaturated essential fatty acids (polyunsaturates) that are particularly important for brain development and function. They are also beneficial for heart health. The best food sources are oily fish, but they are also found in flaxseeds, nuts and seeds.

Oppositional Defiance Disorder - European description:
conduct seen in children below 10 years of age characterised by markedly defiant, disobedient or provocative behaviour.

Oppositional Defiance Disorder - American description:
a pattern of hostile, negative, defiant behavour lasting at least 6 months, during which four of the following occur:- often loses temper, often argues with adults, often actively defies or refuses to comply with requests/rules, often deliberately annoys others, often blames others for his/her mistakes, is easily annoyed, is often angry, is often spiteful.

Otoacoustic Emission Tests
a hearing test of inner ear function.

Otoscope
the device used by doctors for looking in the ear.

Paliocortex
one of the more primitive (older) types of the outer layer of the brain (cortex).

Partially hydrogenated fats
similar to hydrogenated fats (see glossary entry), and another important dietary source of harmful 'trans' fats.

Peripheral nerves
nerves that leave the brain/brainstem/spinal cord.

Peripheral nervous system
the nervous system is divided in the central nervous system – brain/brainstem/spinal cord – and the peripheral nervous system – all the nerves that leave or enter the central nervous system.

Peripheral testing
the testing of the nerves that leave the spinal cord to supply the arms and legs principally.

Phospholipids
a fatty component of the cell wall.

Phytochemicals
literally 'plant chemicals'. Beneficial nutrients found in plant-based foods such as fruit, vegetables, nuts and seeds.

Polysaccharide
a chain made up of individual sugar units.

Prebiotic
non-digestible compounds added to foods and food supplements, to 'feed' the beneficial 'friendly bacteria' in the human gut.

Prefrontal cortex
a large area (in humans) at the front of the brain.

Probiotic
the beneficial 'friendly bacteria' that inhabit the gut.

Prosody
the musical quality of language, as opposed to a flat monotone.

Prostaglandins
a member of a group of fats made from omega -3 and -6.

Protein
a nutrient needed for body growth, maintenance and repair.

Psychometric tests
tests to measure brain function.

PUFA
polyunsaturated fatty acid.

GLOSSARY

Ritalin
a trade name for Methylphenidate Hydrochloride, a central nervous system stimulant used in the "treatment" of ADHD.

Saturated fat
a class of fat, usually solid at room temperature, found mainly in animal products such as meat, eggs and dairy products. Has the effect of raising the level of 'bad' LDL cholesterol.

Savant ability
an extraordinary skill/ability e.g. the ability to remember pages of telephone numbers or the ability to say on which day a persons birthday will fall in any given year.

Schizophrenia
mental illness characterized by impairments in the perception or expression of reality, most commonly manifesting as auditory hallucinations (hearing voices), paranoid or bizarre delusions (false beliefs) or disorganized speech and thinking.

Sensory integration
the blending of sensory input into the body so that it becomes meaningful.

Serotonin
a neurotransmitter believed to play an important role in the regulation of mood, sleep, vomiting, sexuality and appetite.

Sodium chloride
common table salt.

Spindle cells (von Economo cells)
special brain cells (nerves) that develop (principally) four months after birth in humans: they are only found in the brains of the great apes, Man, whales, certain dolphins, manatee and elephants. It is considered that

these cells and the development of the prefrontal cortex (the front of the brain) is what makes us truly human.

Statemented
the 1993 Education Act (UK) provided a code of practice giving guidance on how to identify and assess the special educational needs (SEN) of children: if it is felt that a child has SEN, then a formal request can be made to have the child statemented, which if formally accepted will ensure that the child's needs are met.

Synaesthesia
a condition in which sensory experiences are misinterpreted in the brain so that the sufferer may taste words or feel colours.

Synaptogenesis
the forming of synapses (gaps) between neurons (brain cells) across which chemical messages can pass.

Syndrome
a collection of signs and symptoms that appear together.

Temporal sequencing
fitting events into a time frame.

Titubation
rocking to and fro.

Tourette's syndrome
generally considered to be a condition in which a tic (involuntary movement) is associated with the sufferer swearing uncontrollably: however, minor aspects of it appear in so many children in the form of excessive blinking, grimacing or throat clearing for it to be considered a normal aspect of development.

Trans fats
a class of fats with similar negative health effects to saturated fats. Hydrogenated and partially hydrogenated

fats and oils are their main source in the diet, but they are also naturally found in smaller amounts in animal products.

Tympanometry tests
special hearing tests which assess how well the ear-drum and middle ear is functioning.

Vagal brake
one way in which the brain controls the heart rate, blood pressure and respiration rate.

Ventouse
an assisted birth using suction to pull the baby through the birth canal.

von Economo neurons
see Spindle cells.

Made in the USA
Charleston, SC
24 November 2011